THE PHILOSOPHY

OF

SCHOOL MANAGEMENT

BY

ARNOLD TOMPKINS

AUTHOR OF "THE PHILOSOPHY OF TEACHING" AND "THE SCIENCE
OF DISCOURSE"

The School is an organic, spiritual unity. — W. A. JONES

GINN & COMPANY

BOSTON · NEW YORK · CHICAGO · LONDON

The Athenæum Press

GINN & COMPANY · PRO-
PRIETORS · BOSTON · U.S.A.

PREFACE.

The nucleus of the following discussion appeared as a chapter in the first edition of "The Philosophy of Teaching." It is now expanded into a companion volume, with a more fundamental setting than at first given; and thus with a scope extended to include management from the kindergarten to the university. Those who wish the easier and the more practical discussion will find it beginning on page 67. It is thought, however, that a patient development from the first will be most satisfactory in the end.

The spirit of the book is clearly traceable to contact with W. A. JONES, first president of the Indiana State Normal School. Had it not been for the influence of his class work and his daily practice in management, this book would, perhaps, not have been written; and I can but wish it were a more worthy monument to the memory of the man whose potent ideas stimulated so many to earnest effort in planting fundamental educational doctrines. For wise counsel in the general treatment of the subject I am ever grateful to L. H. JONES, Superintendent of Schools, Cleveland, Ohio.

ARNOLD TOMPKINS.

Chicago, Illinois,
    May 10, 1895.

CONTENTS.

CONTENTS.

INTRODUCTION.

THE teaching process having been considered in "The Philosophy of Teaching," it is now in order to consider the school as an organized means in making that process effective.

To make this discussion of the most practical service, it must reduce the complex school process to the unity of a single principle, to a universal law of management; hence the "Philosophy of Management." It is impossible, as well as undesirable, to prescribe a complete list of specific duties. The wisest economy is to make clear the one principle which has power to take care of all individual cases; and the deeper the principle, the greater the power and the economy. Besides, specific rules deaden and enslave, while a universal law guides and inspires with a consciousness of freedom and power.

A catalogue of "do's" and "do not's" may serve the mere operative in a factory, where the material conditions remain fixed; but the teacher, with whom the conditions are perpetually varying, must be guided by a principle which tact and ingenuity may apply to each new case as it arises. Thus only can the teacher move with certainty and precision; while the application of unvarying rules to varying conditions is the prolific source of error and confusion. A fundamental principle — that is, a principle inherent in all the facts under consideration — has not only the greatest economic breadth of application by including the whole system of facts, but insures the greater certainty in dealing with any one of the facts in the system; because universal truth is also the essential truth.

The teacher, therefore, who would seek skill in the art of school management, must ground himself well in the underlying principle; for skilful practice implies sound theory. It is unsafe, as well as illogical, to set theory over against practice, as if the more of one the less of the other. School management is a process, and the theory of it is the theory of a practice. The two are organically one, — two sides of the same process, the process in thought and the process in external realization. Theory is practice in thought; practice is theory emerging from thought. The one is the process in idea, the other the idea in process. The idea cannot go forth in process till it is first formed in mind; hence every one who practices must have a theory of some kind ; and, other things equal, the practice will be good to the degree of excellence in the theory. The more perfectly the school is held in mind as an organic process, the more perfectly may the process be realized in the school. And the most perfect form of the school process in thought is that of philosophy, — the form which holds all the complex elements of the process in the grasp of a universal law.

But sound theory does not insure successful practice. Tact and common sense have a large, if not the largest, share in the result. Principles cannot apply themselves; there is always supposed to be a teacher who adjusts law to a given case. Tact, the power to touch an instance with a law, is personal and private, and cannot be supplied by a book on theory, — or on practice either, for that matter. This fact is overlooked by those who clamor for the practical in the form of rules and recipes. No rule can be made to fit the case before it arises. If a teacher could be told how to manage a boy in a given offence, — a boy of given age, disposition, temperament, home training of a specific kind, etc., etc., to color of hair and eyes, — it would be useless, since this case can never arise again. There is a realm of immediate and personal responsibility touching each new case as it arises, which cannot be shifted to the side of theory; and this is the realm of skill in the teacher. Unsound theory cannot work; sound theory may not, because it may have to work through imperfect instrumentalities. Let those, therefore, who are disposed to condemn certain theories, withhold judgment till having proved their skill by successfully operating under other principles. It is always possible for those who fail in following one theory to fail under all others. Hence this book, while announcing so positively the value of a universal principle, and developing the idea with earnest conviction, does not hope for satisfactory practice from all who should be thus indoctrinated. All that can be done is to supply the indispensable guiding thought, in light of which successful management is possible. After all, the individual teacher, knowing his own peculiarities, and the particular circumstances under which he operates, must work out his own salvation with fear and trembling.

But the saddest admission to be made is that both theory and art may fail. Given both the science and the skill of management as perfect as could be expected within the limits of human nature, and there are cases which resist all effort, be it ever so wise, patient, and persistent. Some pupils, through heredity, and home and street life, resist to the last the art of the divinely gifted teacher operating on the soundest principles. The school organization is a power for good, but it need surprise no one that it cannot regenerate on the spot every specimen of humanity that comes within its influence. The State has been operating with imposing machinery for ages; but lo! we have the bad citizen with us always. The Church, with its manifold auxiliaries, works with ceaseless industry and inspired zeal to save fallen man, but man is still fallen. Social science, in the vigor, zeal, and hope of youth, has still set the millennium in the distant future. In the long run all of these worthy and heroic efforts are for progress; but they must tolerate evil a while longer, trusting to the measured, peaceful course of time to prove that "through the ages one increasing purpose runs." The school, as a means of ameliorating the condition of man, is grounded in sound faith, distinctly pronounced, and justifiable by its fruits. Social Science, the Church, the State, and the Family, with all their confusion of differences in theory, in creeds, and constitutions, do verily believe the school a power unto righteousness. This charge let the teacher accept in good faith, and put one more shoulder to the wheel of universal progress; but not as a contract to bring at once all the discordant elements resisting the other institutions into one peaceful and harmonious school life. The teacher should not be expected to manage what all the other organizations, especially the family, fail to manage.

If any teacher should take the foregoing as an excuse for anything less than the wisest, the most persistent, and the most sympathetic effort to bring the resisting elements into the unity of school life, and thus save the pupil through unity with his own higher life, I should wish the admission had been suppressed. The teacher must accept the largest responsibility, and measure up to it as fully as possible; yet he should not die in despair because all imperfections in the world are not to be buried with him. This admission of the impotency of theory and art to deal effectively at once with certain conditions and pupils generally found in all schools, is made as the saving clause for those intensely earnest and sensitive teachers who feel conscience-stricken because some stubborn blood globule holds out against all wise and skilful effort. Is there not a limit somewhere to the teacher's responsibility? Even the great Teacher was forced to exclaim, "O Jerusalem, Jerusalem, thou that killest the prophets, and stonest them which are sent unto thee, how often would I have gathered thy children together, even as a hen gathereth her chickens under her wings, and ye would not!" Even so; they would not, and He could not. If they still will not, how can we?

SCHOOL MANAGEMENT.

THE FUNDAMENTAL LAW.

A SCHOOL is quite a complex object, for it includes teachers, pupils, parents, officers, tax-payers, funds, houses, and apparatus. These diverse parts exist in unity, since they co-operate to one end under the moving force of a single idea. All the diverse acts of the several factors focus themselves in the one single act for which all the acts are performed. Hence the school is an organic process. It is this process which is to be managed, and for which there must be a fundamental law, — a law which gives unity to the diversity of functions in the manifold parts, — the *Law of Unity*.

This is obviously the law of any organism whatever. An organism can have no other ; but this law needs detailed specification to appear as the working power in school management. In defining the law to this end, it must first be observed that the law has its sanction : —

Within the Organism Itself. — The law of the school is inherent in the school, and not externally imposed. The botanist may discover laws of growth in the blade of grass, but he cannot legislate for it. The physiologist may announce laws for the circulation of the blood, but he cannot dictate those laws. The law of an organism is its own inherent energy moving forward, by variety of functions in unity, to realize the end which called forth the organism. Laws cannot be imposed upon it; external legislation cannot control its action. The solar system moves on in the way appointed by its own constitution.

This is all plain enough, but it does seem, in the case of social organisms, — objects of man's fixing, — that laws are injected from without by those who set up the organization. A second thought will reveal here also the inherence of law, and that what man does is but external manipulation in obedience to inner law. However much man may fix up plans for any form of social regeneration, things plod on in their own seemingly stubborn way, in obedience to their own nature and destiny. All the learning and legislation of a nation cannot change at will the current of life in a single city; and all helpfully done must be done in obedience to its own inherent law of development. The State itself proclaims what laws to write in the books for its own governing; and it is obedient to them because they are its inward laws outwardly manifested. There is, however, a widely extended theory to the contrary, — a theory which Herbert Spencer combats in the following paragraph from his " Social Statics ": —

"Practically, if not professedly, they (the disciples of Bentham) hold, with Thrasymachus, that nothing is in-

trinsically right or wrong, but that it becomes either by
the dictum of the State. If we are to credit them,
government determines what shall be morality, and not
morality what shall be government. They believe in no
oracular principle by whose yea or nay we may be guided;
their Delphi is the House of Commons. By their account
man lives and moves and has his being by legislative
permit. His freedom to do this or that is not natural,
but conferred. The question, Has the citizen any claim
to the work of his hands? can be decided only by parlia-
mentary division. If 'the ayes have it,' he has; if 'the
noes,' he has not."

Man may discover, and formulate in statutes, laws in
organizations, but the laws are still in the organizations,
ready to challenge the fictions of man's ordaining. Laws
and statutes are not the same; they may even be antagonistic, and the law compelled to disown the statute. The
law of the school which concerns us here is not the school
law found in the statute books, but the inherent nature
of the school as legislating for itself; as giving law to all
factors and functions, even to school law itself.

But within this large and complex organism all parts
and phases are not equally authoritative. The law which
binds in unity does not inhere in the external, objective,
and fixed parts, but must be sought: —

Within the Organism as a Spiritual Process. — The
fundamental law of the school is implied in the statement that "the school is an organic spiritual unity."
It is not merely the co-operation of objective and appar-

ently fixed factors, but a movement of life through external forms back to life again.   The law is not to be found
in the material, obtrusive, objective, and stationary factors
in the process ; but within the inner life which moves
the organism to the realization of its purpose, — in the
spirit which makes alive to its work the apparent
organism, but not in the apparent organism.

Everything exists in idea, in life and thought, before
it can exist in objective reality; and the function of such
objective thing is to realize the idea which created it.
Such is the circle of its life and the law of its being.
The idea rapid transit brought forth the railroad, and
the railroad in turn must bring forth rapid transit.   The
railroad must relieve the pressure of life which creates
it; but this pressure is a constant force, and the railroad
is being perpetually created and held to the work of
relieving the pressure.   The idea by which it is realized
must in turn be realized by it.   Hence the railroad is
not a fixed, dead, objective something, but a constant
going out and returning to life; it is life.   The objective
thing cut loose from the life process is not a railroad; it
vanishes into nothing when cut from its spiritual moorings.   A railroad is not merely the external organization
of material parts, but a circle of life, which is its reality
and its law.

The idea of developing the child by a systematic teaching process brings forth the objective school; and this
in turn must bring forth the development of the child.
The objective school must answer back to the life which

supports it. It stands as the middle term in a series, — between an idea and its realization; but it takes the whole series to constitute the school. The objective, fixed something called the school, is only a phase in the process, and is nothing apart from that process. It exists in and through realizing the idea by which it itself is realized. The real school is the whole process, not merely the objective phase of it; it is the constant outgoing of life through an external mediating agency back to life. This circle, again, and not merely the external organization of fixed parts, is its reality and its law.

And this school process is still more complex. The idea which originates the school has two phases, — one that of a felt *need* for something to remove the limitations of life, and the other that of *instruction* as a means of removing the limitations. The idea originating the external organization *purposes* the freedom of the individual through *instruction*. These are the elements of the school in idea; neither can be omitted, nor can they arise in any other order. Instruction cannot be conceived without the idea of an end to be realized; and the idea of an external school cannot arise except under the thought of instruction. Each may exist in thought without the succeeding, but not without the preceding; which shows that the subjective school is a movement in the direction named, — purpose, instruction, external organization.

The foregoing elements of the school in idea reverse themselves in the process of realization; for then the external organization comes first, after which instruction is given, and then the purpose is realized. Neither can this order be reversed. The purpose cannot be realized without instruction, and the instruction cannot be given without organized means to that end. And these three phases of school can exist only on the foregoing three as a basis. Besides, they must exist in the reverse order, — are logically conditioned in that order. The first in idea is last in objective reality. An idea always reverses the order of its elements in the process of becoming external; the beginning becomes the end; "the first shall be last, and the last shall be first," as appears in the following diagram of the school process: —

	THE IDEA SCHOOL becoming	1. Purpose, or Need.
		2. Instruction.
THE SCHOOL PROCESS.		3. Organization — Management.
	THE REAL SCHOOL.	4. Organization — Management.
		5. Instruction.
		6. Purpose, or Need, Realized.

Thus the objective school organization, both as idea and as objective reality, is the hinging-point on which the ideas, purpose, and instruction fold back upon themselves as actualized instruction and purpose. The ideal purpose and method of instruction form the subject-matter in "The Philosophy of Teaching." The hinging-point, through which purpose and instruction are turned back realized, is the subject-matter for "School-Management;"

and the fundamental law of school management is disclosed in the fact that the subject to be treated is a hinging-point in the school process, and not a thing in and of itself.

Thus we are brought to the fact of supreme practical importance; namely, that the fundamental law controlling the school as an external organization cannot be dictated by that organization, but has its origin in the process taken as a whole. While the law must arise from within, as shown at the outset, yet the law does not get its authority from any part, but from the school as a whole, taken in its entire circle of activity. The part, such as the external organization, with which management has to do, receives its law from the whole. The law of the school is its informing life, its inherent nature, which finds expression in the objective something with which school management has to deal. All the organic factors of the external organization, including the school law itself, must be tested by an idea which is antecedent to, and which logically conditions, the external and objective school

The external organization, instead of dictating the law, may even be in opposition to the law. Even the statute embodying school law may be antagonistic to the law of the school. School directors, under a false sense of economy, sometimes lower the tax levy and shorten the school term. This is done by permission of the school law but in opposition to the law of the school. In faithful execution of the school law, it may be necessary to crowd sixty pupils into the care of one teacher; but the idea which creates the school has not its freedom under such conditions. Under substantially the same conditions different States have different laws regulating the supply of books to pupils. These laws cannot all be best; and in so declaring we recognize something inherent in the school by which the school law itself is to be tested. Without such recognition school questions could not be argued. While never agreeing as to what is best in school organization and law, we do tacitly agree always that there is a best, if we could but discover it, and that this best is determined by something inherent in the nature of the school underlying external organization.

It thus appears that the established order is not the ethical order. The fugitive slave law is rendered null and void by the inner law. History is a record of conflicts between the ideal and inner truth of things, and external forms which were fixed by custom and law. There is a perennial strife between those who are loyal to forms as against the idea, and those who are loyal to the idea as against the form. There are those who seem to think that the external condition of things is the law, and therefore unassailable. Especially prone to hold this view are those who are a part of the fixed system. It seems to be the order, when a school system becomes fixed and crystallized, for those who form a part of the system to plead the fixed order as the ethical order, and to brand as iconoclasts or anarchists those who hold that the idea must not be violated.

" Hence every moral and social advance has to fight its way not merely against the bad who oppose all order, but against the traditionally good, who believe that the social order is constant, and that what has been the ideal adjustment in the past must remain the ideal of conduct for all time. These conscientious but short-sighted conservatives are always more bitter and powerful opponents of the new ideal than the unprincipled rabble. The worst enemy of the better is the good. It was the constituted authorities, the conservative aristocracy of Athens, not the lawless and irreligious masses, who condemned Socrates to drink the hemlock. It was the Scribes and the Pharisees and the chief priests and the principal men of Jerusalem who crucified Jesus. . . .

"The higher form of this struggle comes between the law as the representative of the existing order, — or rather of the order which existed when the law was framed, — and the individuals who see the vision of the better order that is about to be, and demand institutions, customs, standards, duties, liberties large enough to meet the requirement of the social order that has come into being since the law was made, or stands ready to come as soon as the hard crust of the old order can be broken so as to give the new life room. Here society is behind the individual, and is trying to hold him back. Thus the average good man is equally at war with the bad man who is below him, and the progressively good man who is above him. The reformer and the criminal are about equally obnoxious to the man of average goodness and intelligence. The prophets and the betrayers of their country are equally odious, and promis-cuously stoned. The Saviour is crucified between two thieves." [1]

The forms through which life realizes itself, whether school, family, society, church, or state, tend to fix them-selves, and to check the life which grows through them. This is natural and inevitable. A considerable part of man's effort must be spent in readjusting the forms of life to the growing conditions of life. Man lives in advance of the customs of society, the laws of the state, the creeds of the church, and the methods and statutes of the school. When the tension becomes too great, as it does naturally and periodically, the old forms must be readjusted, or new ones substituted. It will be evolution or revolution. To avoid conflict and bondage, forms should grow with the growing life. The radical sunders old forms before the life is ready for the new; the con-servative clings to old forms after they are outgrown; the serpent shows more wisdom in shedding the old skin through forming the new. One of the serious problems of school management is how to shed modes, forms, and customs through forming the new, that no violence may be done in the transition. The iconoclast would not have to break our idols, and with them our faith, if he would spend his time in preparing us to worship better things. The wisdom of the serpent in these matters would be the harmlessness of the dove.

But in making the change from the old to the new,

[1] Social Theology, — Dr. HYDE.

what is and what has been in external organization, while serving as a basis of action, can never be the advancing light — can never reveal what ought to be. The history of education is usually justified in a teacher's course, on the ground that in knowing what has been, it is known what ought to be. But the history of education cannot be read except in light of the unrealized ideal. History shows how far the idea has succeeded in realizing itself, and this is vital to the teacher; but to learn what has been, in order to find in such external a standard for imitation, is the servitude of form, and not the freedom of an idea. The best text-book on a given subject cannot be made by averaging texts already made; and the best one existing cannot be excelled without recognizing an ideal beyond anything accomplished. To study school systems with a view to finding a standard in the average best thing, is to keep the standard from advancing. If progress is to be made, the standard must be created and set up in advance of anything realized. Not what is, but what ought to be, is the paramount question. The law of the school requires that the teacher struggle against environment and existing forms to a fuller realization of the idea than has yet been attained. The strongest tension possible must be maintained up to the risk of breaking with the forms and environment in which the life is rooted. This law of school life is the universal law of living, which holds that the real must continually yield to the ideal as it presses onward to realize itself.

This tension between the real and the ideal reveals itself clearly in the two classes of educational theorists and practitioners: those who construct the system *a priori*, and those who construct it *a posteriori*, — from the causal force of an idea, and from experience. The first, in the extreme type, ignore the concrete conditions, and build an educational Utopia; the second, in the extreme, see nothing but the concrete fixed conditions, and sink below the best already attained. Of the first type there are very few; and even their mistakes are inspiringly helpful; of the second, and of those tending that way, is the great body of the profession, and with them rests the professional crimes against childhood. The crime of all crimes, so frequently committed by teachers and superintendents, is that of comfortably and safely adjusting to existing conditions and prevailing sentiments among those for whom they labor. Whether a teacher be inspired by the idea, so that he presses onward towards its realization, or whether simply wise in harmoniously fitting into prevailing modes and opinions, determines, more than any other one thing, whether he bless or blight the life he is supposed to save. It is worthy of note that those teachers put down in the world's history for eminent service have been inspired with an idea which pressed firmly and constantly against existing conditions; while others have gone into hibernation to spend as securely and comfortably as possible the winter of their professional lives. Of course one must not break with his environment, for to do so would be to lose his usefulness; but if he levels to it, he has no usefulness to lose. What needs to be insisted on is the presence of an inner law, which must constantly re-shape and mould the external condition of things, on the basis of the existing condition of things. Every ideal must rise upon the real to which it is in bondage. Outer forms and laws are but stepping-stones of the living idea, which constructs for itself new stepping-stones as they are needed.

Thus the broadest requirement made by the fundamental law of the school is that the organization be adjusted to the demand of the ideal; that it never be regarded as fixed and an end; but that it be a perfect means standing between ideal purpose and instruction on the one hand, and realized instruction and purpose on the other, — the teaching process in idea, and the teaching process in objective reality. A school organization is tested by ascertaining how fully the thought and purpose of those in whom the organization rests has been realized by its agency. Of course it is of first importance to have a high ideal in the teaching process; but this ideal belongs to the philosophy of teaching, and we are here concerned only with its adequate realization through the school as an external means.

Thus the real school, from which law emanates, is mind in effort to unfold mind; and not the school-house and appliances, school officers and school law. This effort binds into a school, citizens, parents, officers, teachers, and pupils. These minds may not be actively making such effort in order that there be a school, but they must be permanently disposed to make it. The school exists during vacation. A university does not vanish at commencement. A state university is a certain disposition in the minds of the state, — a spiritual power to act through external agencies in a specified process of instruction. The whole external organization falls to pieces in a moment when such disposition is withdrawn. Then the school-house is no longer a school-house; a trustee no longer a trustee; the teacher ceases to be a teacher. Thus again it appears that the objective school, cut loose from its spiritual moorings, vanishes. This cannot be too often insisted upon, for we are so much accustomed to feel that the external, objective, and perhaps material something is the reality; and that therefore laws and principles of operation inhere in it, and are to be deduced from it. We are quite strictly materialists in school management; setting objective and fixed forms and rules hard and fast over against a growing and pulsating life.

Thus the broadest aspect of the law of unity requires the circle from the ideal through the external organization to the real—the life circle—to be kept intact; that everything in the external organization be kept in movement to the realization of an ideal; that the end always dominate the means and never be dominated by it. In closest statement the unity is that of the ideal and the real; and the meaning of the law is that the external organization must be true to this unity, and not set up one of its own.

But the school conceived merely as "an organic spiritual

unity" is too vague and general to have working value, and must be reduced to lower terms: —

In the Spiritual Unity of Teacher and Pupil. — This seems to be the spiritual centre out of which issues all law, and to which all instrumentalities co-operate; for it is here that the miracle of changing the ideal into the real is wrought. The co-operation of these two factors accomplishes the end for which the whole system exists. Teacher and pupil, in co-operative touch to the end for which the school exists, of themselves constitute the school. A thumb-bell may be a part of the organization; but the change from the ideal to the real is not in its co-operation with any other organ. The change can take place, and the school can exist without it. A clock and a blackboard may be parts of the school machinery; but the teaching process can go on without them, and the school is not destroyed by their removal. The co-operation of the school-house is not the teaching process, and the school can exist with a Mark Hopkins on one end of a log and a Garfield on the other. Drawing more nearly to the school, and yet the teaching process can exist without gymnasium, laboratory, or library. The co-operation of neither of these with any other constitutes the process, and the efficiency of the organization cannot be tested therein. Director, trustee, county superintendent, state superintendent, and national commissioner of education are useful members, but the school can exist in idea, as it has done in fact, without them. The co-operation of either of them with any other factor is not the teaching process, and a school system cannot be tested in the work of either. It would at first seem that if the public fund and tax-payer were removed, the bottom would fall out of the institution; but it is not so. School must keep; the sentiment is too deeply rooted to be baffled by trifling inconveniences through lack of organized fund, or hierarchy of officers, or school-house with all the wealth of modern appliances. Even if the parent were removed, the school would still operate; for a time, at least; as long as necessary.

But the process vanishes if either teacher or pupil be dropped. These two in co-operative unity constitute a school, and the law is to be tested in their organic unity. All other parts of the organism work their way down to this unity through these two factors. The prolonged and heroic effort States have made in organizing a school fund is to bring teacher and pupil together under the most favorable conditions of co-operation. The Commissioner of Education must find his way through the long line of forces down to the touch of teacher with pupil. Library, laboratory, and gymnasium are but unifying agencies between teacher and pupil; and the value of thumb-bell or clock, eraser or wall map, is tested by the influence exerted on the unity of teacher with pupil. Thus the school is quite a complex, but closely integrated, process. Every act performed, however remote, finds its way to the unity described; and is there tested. When the director fails to supply good fuel, or the trustee a good blackboard, the unity is weakened. When the county superintendent gives license to a teacher, or a trustee selects one, the value of the act will be tested in the unity of teacher and pupil in the teaching act. The State Superintendent renders a decision, and it ultimately shows itself in the concrete teaching process, — in the unity of mind with mind in the teaching act. The teacher fails to prepare the lesson, and the detrimental result is found when his mind fails to come into unity with that of the pupil on the topic under consideration.

Behavior or conduct in school, whether on the part of the teacher, parent, pupil, or school officer, is the way one bears himself in reference to this vital touch of mind with mind in the act of instruction. A right act in school is one which secures, or tends to secure, unity between the mind of the teacher and the pupil in the teaching process; while a wrong act is one which destroys, or tends to destroy, such unity. School management is the process by which all the acts of all the agents constituting the organism are brought into the unity of the one act above described. The law of the school, therefore, as an external organism, requires unity to the vital contro of its manifold and complex parts. Thus, besides the school process as a whole, as at first described, and of which the external organization is a link, there is another organic process in the objective school, — a working together of all its complex parts to a point in the school process as a whole.

The character of the unity between teacher and pupil further specifies the law. The two are one in the teach-

.2

ing process; for in teaching, whatever thought, sentiment, or resolution the teacher would stimulate in the pupil's mind, he must first have in his own consciousness. While causing the pupil to think the colors of the rainbow, the teacher must think them; and if the pupil's heart is to leap up when he beholds "a rainbow in the sky," the teacher's must leap with it. And the resolution and tendency to higher life expected in the pupil from the rainbow study must be the resolution and tendency of his own life under that study. Thus, in all teaching there is a point of identity of consciousness between teacher and pupil. This identity of consciousness is the centre of the system, and it is this which management is to secure. Suppose the teacher, in teaching "Paul Revere's Ride," be in the inspired mood to which his pupil is to be brought, good management will bring the pupil into unity with the teacher's inspiration; and the extent to which the pupil falls short, barring the question of his ability, must be put to the score of bad management somewhere in the system. At the moment of that effort on the part of the teacher, the whole school system, out to its remotest limits, stands pledged to the unity of inspiration of teacher and pupil in the poem under con-sideration. The tax-payer is toiling for it; the Commissioner of Education is issuing his report to that end; the State Superintendent is interpreting the law to strengthen the work in hand; the county superintendent is issuing orders for the good of the cause ; and the school-house, with its library, gymnasium, wall-map, blackboard, crayon, pointer, and eraser, marshals all its forces to the issue. The stove, the desks, the table, the curtains at the window, — all are focusing their energy at the moment to bring the pupil's inspiration up to that of the teacher's. Even the Governor and the President of the United States stand in constant and vital touch with the effort to arouse the pupil to the level of the teacher. Thus, at any moment, the school consists of the active, purposed influences which combine to draw the pupil into unity with the teacher in the teaching act. Again the school appears not to be a fixed something, but a living, moving thing in the process of realizing an idea. The school is a complex of functions, bringing teacher and pupil into co-operation.

But while in the teaching act there is a point of identity between teacher and pupil, there is the important difference which makes the act of one teaching and that of the other learning. They are really thinking about different things. The point of subject-matter in which the two are to unite is old to the teacher; and at the time merely reproduced in idea in order to awaken the same in tho mind of the pupil. The teacher in the act of teaching is really thinking of the pupil's experience, while the pupil is thinking about the subject under consideration. The subject being old to the teacher, and merely reproduced in idea to guide in stimulating the pupil to realize the same, the teacher turns his effort to the experience of the pupil in the act of learning; and with this further difference, that the teacher is conscious of the value of the experience of the pupil in terms of his unfolding life. What the teacher should be really conscious of is the process of growth on the part of the pupil in the act of fostering it. In teaching, the true teacher lives in the life of the pupil. If each lesson does not change the life of the pupil, no reason can be assigned for giving it; and if this be true, the teacher must be conscious of the change made in the act of making it; or the blind will be leading the blind. Hence the teacher must hold the pupil's life in his grasp in each act of teaching, — his whole life, for each lesson touches it from its centre to its circumference. Now, this good of life, immediate and remote, the pupil cannot be conscious of; if so, he could be his own teacher. In teaching, then, the pupil puts his effort on the subject-matter, while the teacher puts his effort on the growing life of the pupil, through his experiences with the subject-matter. The teacher holds in idea the aim, and the experiences by which the aim is realized; and at the same time the pupil has the real experiences and thus realizes the aim. Thus we have reached the point where the miracle is wrought, — the change from the ideal to the real, for which the organized system stands. And thus, too, while drawing differences between teacher and pupil, we have reached a more fundamental likeness, — a likeness in purpose and effort, which combine the two into the unity which makes the school. We have already seen that these two factors are the essential ones in the school process; that they really constitute the school.

They form the school in the unity of purpose and effort to realize the life of the pupil. Consciously or unconsciously, the pupil is making an effort to realize his possibilities, and the teacher is uniting with him in the effort. In this unity of effort of the two we have the school in its simplest and most concrete form; but in the larger sense, the school consists of all the minds making effort with the pupil in his development. Thus it appears again that the school is a spiritual unity, consisting of minds in effort to unfold mind. Minds permanently disposed to make such effort is the school, in repose or quiescent; but when the effort is active, we have the school in process.

But in all this the teacher, while not vanishing, as did the thumb-bell, is reduced to the secondary position of instrument; and in last analysis we are forced to locate the law simply: —

Within the Spiritual Unity of the Pupil Himself. — This is the unity of the pupil's real and ideal self; or rather, the school is the tension between the two. Reaching inward through all the forms and process of the complex school system, this tension is found as the last and the abiding force; and moving outward from this centre, it may be seen determining and drawing all instrumentalities to the infinite work of releasing the tension, which is constantly renewed. The student, directly or indirectly, consciously or unconsciously, creates the school as external organization. This is quite obvious in the case of mature students. The first schools were made by the students themselves. Schools for children came later, and were created in sympathy for them, — created as they would have done for themselves, had they been conscious of their needs. In any case it is the student who virtually organizes instrumentalities for his own development. Those who join with him in effort are only instrumentally connected; they are not the primary motive in the process. When a university is founded, it is on the assumption of a basis in the purpose, latent or active, in a number who are striving for improvement. Students might create, support and manage the institution by which they themselves are taught, as is done in a church by its members. In this case it is evident that the spirit of the student is the basis of the school; but it is no less so when they accept agencies prepared on the assumption that they will make those agencies their own.

And here we have come upon the most specific and vital principle of school management, — one which must be carried forward throughout the discussion. A school is firmly grounded when it is conscious of itself, if we may think of it so, — that is, when the objective school is held by the pupil as arising out of his own life; when seen as truly himself, and not the will of another; when he does not feel that it is something set over against himself, but that it is himself projected in that form for his own self-realization. This means that school administration should be entirely democratic; that is, no arbitrary will must displace the pupil's obedience to himself as objectified in the school. At first, of course, he may not be able to see himself as the law, except in detail; but to gradually reveal the fact to him that he is the school, to which his conduct must conform, is the very triumph of management. The school is never stable unless it rests in the pupil's adoption of it as his law; in this the school has its fullest and firmest reality.

It is obvious from the foregoing that the worst stroke of management imaginable is one which assails the reality of the school; and it usually takes this shape. The teacher, or it may be those administering affairs, says to pupils, in word or bearing, "I am running an institution here, of which you are members by grace. Yes, come to think of it, I am really glad of your presence, and will take it as a personal favor for you to patronize my establishment, for by this I gain my livelihood. Of course, I will expect to recompense you with whatever favors I may be able to bestow, — such as securing positions in store or workshop; and it may be that if you remain long enough, and make the obligation great enough, I may reward you with a position in my school, to which you will have been so disinterestedly loyal. But if there is disorder here, — if you in any way interfere with the smooth running of my business, — beware of my right arm. All rights, privileges, and immunities are vested in me; I make and execute the law. When you touch the school, you touch my personal affairs. Beware, I say; vengeance is mine." In this attitude a school may be crushed into seeming good order, but it is the worst of disorder; not only because students and teacher are sundered, but because the organization is shifted from its real basis, and the unity of the student's life with it is broken.

From this it must not be inferred that the management of the school must be turned over to the whims and caprices of the students, but that all things be done from the standpoint that the student, constantly setting up in thought the organization for his own development, is the school.   Hence, negatively, management must do nothing to forbid the pupil from projecting his own rational nature as the school; and, positively, must do everything possible to enable the pupil to see the school as his own life, and to render obedience to its laws as to the laws of his own nature.   The citizen reads the enactment of the state against theft, and discerns in it nothing but the requirement of his own nature, and renders obedience to it as his true self objectified.   In this attitude he is free, for he renders obedience only to himself; whereas, if the law is something foreign to him, and thus imposed upon him, he is a slave to external requirement. The free citizen, the free state, the free country, mean only the freedom of self-obedience of the subject, — the obedience of the self to the larger self, — the state. Every individual in the state must come at last to say, with more commendable pride than Louis XIV., "I am the state."   The best state policy is not that which adjusts the tariff, but that which makes every individual conscious of statehood.

And thus the student reads the law of the school against

truancy and the like, and should see these as nothing but the requirements of his own nature, as his own school life, and render obedience to them as his own true self. It may be good, but it cannot be best, for a pupil to obey his teacher. It is a false assumption that he is predisposed to disobey the requirements of the school, and that external authority must enter at once on the work of suppression. The main line of work running through the management of a school is that of developing in the thought of the pupil the laws which are in the school because of his membership in it. This does not require a logical exposition of the theory of the school, but the laws are to be made to appear through the concrete situations of school life. Consultation, formal or informal, on special interests and phases of conduct, is the effective means, even with a class of youngest students. The mere compliment of recognition forestalls opposition and outbreak. But the best result is not the mere matter of order, but the ethical value to the student: he becomes a student of conduct; he is finding the law of conduct in particular cases, and gradually, as he is able, generalizes them into the law of school conduct; and through this the laws of conduct at large will be revealed to him. And more, it is not merely a perception of law, but there is an habitual practice under the law; not merely his expanding theory of ethical conduct, but his expanding free and virtuous life under that theory. He is immediately and directly involved in every case; and it becomes a question of his own practice, and not a scheme to apply to others. No amount of moral teaching in school can be as effective as a rational practice of school management. By it the school is not only made more real and secure, and the immediate condition for instruction provided, but the pupil is thereby brought to the habit of rational self-control, the end of all ends in school work. We should expect, of course, that, if the thing be done fundamentally right, harmony must reign throughout; and that in thus securing one end all other ends will be added.

Instead, therefore, of all the agencies in the school system simply co-operating to the unity of teacher and pupil, the co-operation centres in the pupil, — in the unity between the pupil's real and his ideal self. Hence the teacher, who even stands in vital touch with the pupil, cannot give law to the school. It has already been developed and stated on page 7 "that the fundamental law controlling the school as an external organization cannot be dictated by that organization;" and now it seems that the teacher is a part of that external organization. Teachers, principals, and superintendents, stand in such immediate and vital relation to the process that it is dangerously easy for them to assume arbitrarily the law-giving function, and difficult for them to subject themselves as means to the child as an end. This is the law of justice in the school, and is based on the same distinction as that which Plato, through the character of Socrates, urges on the sophist in searching for the nature of justice. The sophist had declared justice to be the interest of the stronger; but Plato urged that justice always considers the interest of the weaker. He claimed that a shepherd, in the character of a shepherd. conducts himself with reference to the welfare of his sheep, and not in the interest of the shepherd; that a physician, as a physician, is guided by the welfare of his patient, and that in so far as he is guided by money interests, he is a business man and not physician; that a governor of a State, in the character of governor, must act with sole reference to the welfare of his subjects. The teacher, too, has a business side; but in so far as he is teacher, his conduct must be regulated entirely by the welfare of his pupil, and the welfare of the same pupil must control wholly the conduct of superintendent and trustee, in the character of super-intendent and trustee. This truth is so obvious that it seems useless to discuss it; yet this is the criminal point in practice, and the law quite commonly violated, for the motive of self-interest on the part of the teacher or officer, confronts the interest of the pupil. The self-interest of those in the organization to whom the welfare of the child is intrusted is the most formidable obstacle to the law of the school. When some township trustees used school money for their own private ends, they were properly branded criminals; and they fled before the hot wrath of an outraged public to the cooler and more con-genial clime of Canada. But their crime consisted in nothing more than in shortening the school term, and thus preventing so much opportunity on the part of the child. Was there anything more in this crime than the preference of self, as trustee, to the child? Then what an alarming host of criminals in school work! Have you forgotten that other trustee, who, to wield local influences to his own interests, dropped a true and tried teacher of valuable experience for the doubtful and untried one? In both the child was not consulted, and its interests were ignored; both robbed the child. The latter may even have done so much more effectively than the former, through incompetency and the dwarfing influences of bad teaching. Yet the form of their crime was so different that one remains an honored citizen, while the others are the subjects of contempt and ignominy. Both robbed the child, and in this were equally criminal. What we need is a quickened school-conscience to see it so. Whenever a city superintendent chooses the poorer of two teachers because of friendship, or to stand in with certain influences, he could not rob the child more effectively by putting his hand into the treasury, and ought to be hooted to Canada to keep company with his brethren. And so ought the teacher who, for selfish reasons, forgets the child in his eagerness for popularity, that he may control influences which make his calling and election sure. When Lincoln, at a critical period in the war, desired to make a call for soldiers, he was reminded by the politicians that he was a candidate for re-election to the presidency, and that such a call would weaken his prospect. With characteristic devotion, he replied that it was not necessary for him to be re-elected to the presidency, but that it was necessary to save the Union unbroken to the next man who filled the presidential chair. Such must be the spirit of the true teacher,— self-forgetful devotion to those whom he serves.

The other danger is that of forgetting the child in the movement of the complicated machinery. The central process in the pupil must command all the external and remote appliances and processes; but it is uniformly true, and it seems necessarily so, that the teacher, before reaching his freedom in the central law of the school, must pass through some form of bondage to the machinery which conditions his labor. All in all, the school is quite a complex piece of machinery. There are manifold processes to be performed aside from the central one. Teachers must be examined, the coal bought, the house cleaned, the record kept, classes called, and questions asked, — a manifold process so absorbing in variety and interests of detail, so overshadowing the little silent process wherein the miracle is wrought, that the external means become an end in the consciousness of those who teach and manage. Machinery there must be. There must be laws for raising revenue, a school system, school officers, and similar instrumentalities. The record of our early struggle to secure a school fund and a school system is a most worthy one; but it sometimes seems that the greater emphasis given to the system, the more danger there is of forgetting the child. It sometimes becomes a question whether the child can survive the machine. We have just pride in our success in grading schools; but who has not been pained by the fact that the grading often becomes the end, and the child crushed in the process. It often happens that more discussion turns about grading than about the thing really to be done. There cannot be good schools without good grading, but a very poor school may be found where there is good grading. Scarcely anything pertinent is said in boasting of such things. If the contrivance is good, let it be spoken of in terms of the teaching act. No appliance is good so long as it is used as an end. All appliances are good when subordinated to their proper relation and work. One of the most interesting and difficult problems for the superintendent of a school, or a system of schools, whether city, state, or county, is to find his way to the pupil through the complex machinery with which he necessarily labors. The teacher finds his way directly, the superintendent indirectly; but he must find his way, or he is not a superintendent. His life must touch the child, notwithstanding the many agencies that intervene. The long line of appliances and forces standing between him and the child are there only as a means by which he can reach the many; and if he gets himself tangled up in the machinery, he may not reach the child till too late for the rescue.

Thus we have reached the simple but potent truth that the general law of unity of the organism which controls the whole complex school system reduces itself in last analysis to the unity of the pupil's ideal and real self. This is the unity which must never be violated, and which the whole system stands pledged to maintain. In all questions of school organization and management this is the court of ultimate appeal.

This ultimate law of the school appears the more authoritative when we reflect on what has been implied throughout, and incidentally suggested many times; namely, that the law of the school organization is the law of all organizations whatever, whether spiritual or physical. The law applies to the plant and the animal, to the church and the state, as well as to the school. Of course the mechanism, as the watch, differs; for in such the law is externally imposed. But a mechanism is but a means, a phase, in an organism, and is contrived and operated under the same law,— which law works from without. In all cases the law ruling the world is the tension of the ideal and the real,— the striving for unity, peace, and harmony. The real gives the law of truth, and we affirm what a thing is; the ideal proclaims the law of duty, and we affirm what a thing ought to be; having the unity of the two, we announce the thing beautiful. But a thing really *is* not until it is what it *ought* to be, and then it is beautiful; hence truth, beauty, and virtue are phases of the world's movement under the tension of the real and the ideal,— the ultimate energy to which thought can penetrate.

All institutions arise under this strain of ethical impulse which, reduced to its lowest terms, means the unity of the ideal and the real self; all are processes of self-realization. The many-sidedness of life requires different methods of work, and hence different organizations; but whatever the variety of leverage required, the ultimate aim and law of all institutions, whether industrial or sacred, is the same. All days are holy, all work sacred, all institutions divine. Whatever difference there may be between a book on school management and one on the management of any other organization is only a difference in details. While we often try to define the school as distinct from the other institutions, it is much more helpful, because more fundamental, to see how it is in unity with every other. A difference is always at least one remove less fundamental than a likeness.

From one standpoint the school is an offshoot and enlargement of the family, seeking by more effective means to accomplish the same result, — the nurture of the child into the highest type of man or woman. As such, its law must be the same as that of the family. From another view the school is but a specialized function of the industrial world, — an effective means to physical comfort and happiness through the knowledge and virtue which form the basis of the industrial system. But the industrial world seeks more than mere animal welfare, — it is moved by blind impulse or conscious law to the spiritual good of man; and in this the law of the school is the same as the law of the shop. In still another aspect the school is a function of the state, whose sole aim is to harmonize in justice the aggregate efforts of all organizations in their working to realize the supreme good of life. The school, by developing intelligence and ethical virtues, grounds the state firmly, and in return is organized and supported to make its contribution to the common cause of human welfare. It gives and it receives; it supports and is supported; but all this is but one complex effort to realize the ideal of life. Self-realization is the law of both school and state. The church organizes its forces about the relation of man to his Maker, and strives to make man perfect, even as his Father in heaven is perfect; but it has always made the school its intimate ally in every work of regeneration. The problem of both church and school is to bring man ultimately into unity with his destiny, — the ultimate ideal of the human soul. The school is a religious institution; certainly so in its historical origin, and no less so in its ultimate aim.[1]

And thus all institutions arise out of the same truth; namely, that man seeks another self. No one gives law to the others; they are all ways of working out the same problem, — ways growing out of the many-sidedness of the individual. All institutions arise out of the nature of the life of the individual, and must return to that life; all are but methods of realizing the value of human life in the individual. This is the simple law of the great complex social whole. Social science seeks but the formula by which the complex forces in the aggregate of human life best work in unity to the end of righteousness in the individual, — how the whole makes perfect the individuals which constitute the whole.

The whole social machinery is but a complex school system, to bring man out of his present real world into the world of higher truth and reality. In fact, we should

[1] See Philosophy of Teaching, pages 270–275.

scarcely pass the limit of literal language if we should say that the universe itself is such a system; for what do we know of the universe but a nature, an energy, striving through, and by means of, outer forms to a more perfect manifestation of itself? And this energy, so far as man presumes to officiate, or even to comprehend, is what has been stated as the law of the school, and which appears authoritative in having universal validity for all organizations. Even the universe is but a striving after the unity of the real and the potential, of appearance and ultimate reality.

THE LAW EVOLVING THE ORGANISM.

HAVING moved inward through the organism to find the law, the way is prepared to move outward, and study the organism in light of its genesis under the law. Thus the parts and their functions can best be made to appear in their true relations, and the conditions prepared for the active process to be described in the next chapter, — "The Organism in Executing the Law."

The law of unity between the individual's real and ideal self lies back of the formal school organization; and, as before stated, is common to all organizations. It shapes the school as the vital principle shapes the physical organism. The school is the immediate off-spring of the rational nature of the individual; it is that nature externalized. Man, having the power to distinguish between his present attainment and his potential good, takes an active part in his own development. Man is held responsible for shaping his own life. In this dual relation of the individual to himself we have both the teacher and the taught, and therefore the school; for the school is the organic unity between the teacher and the pupil. Teacher and pupil are correlative, twin-born; yea, triple-born, for the school is born with them, being the correlation of the other two. If the school did not thus exist organized in subjective consciousness, it could not exist in objective reality. This fact of self-consciousness, which is the origin and law of the school, is the point of departure in "The Philosophy of Teaching." All managing resolves itself into teaching, and all teaching takes form in managing. The two are the outside and the inside of the same process.

The formal school arises when the function of self-instruction is delegated to another. This other, being farther removed from the pupil's real self, secures a higher tension with that real self. Thus the school, implicit in the nature of the individual, arises in the act of consciousness which differentiates into teacher and taught; and is formally organized when the pupil, or his agents, authorizes another to stand for his ideal. This illustrates again the fact that the school is a projection out of the nature of the individual himself. By his own nature he is pupil to himself as teacher. If this were not true, he could have no other teacher. The school is verily himself; and, as before shown, in rendering obedience to it, he but obeys his own nature.

Again, the school appears to have a like nature with all other institutions, for all are but specializations and externalizations of the life of the individual. For instance, the individual has in himself the disposition, and to a certain extent the physical ability, to protect himself in the rush and violence of city life. He might, by training in courage and pugilistic qualities, and with the proper weapons of self-defence, protect himself; but instead of developing this aspect of his life, he delegates the function of self-defence to a police force, transforming his labor, performed more efficiently in another direction because withdrawing himself from police duty, into the police service of another, through the medium of exchange in the form of city tax. So with the fire department, the board of health, the postal service, the court of justice, the manufactory, the surgical institute, the state, and every possible form of institutional life, — all are but specialized and externalized functions of the individual to the end of more efficient service, secured through some medium of exchange for service of the individual performed in the special direction of his own fitness. By the miracle of institutional and social life the individual transforms himself into the most skilful physician, lawyer, architect, engineer, pilot, minister, or teacher, as he may need; each of these is but the projection of some specialized desire and faculty, to the end of his own more diverse and complete living.

And so the faculty by which the individual instructs himself is made more efficient by giving it specialized objective form in another. Thus the school, and all other institutions, has a subjective origin in the nature, needs, and impulses of the individual. The most immediate and fundamental part of the external school organism, because serving as direct means to the unity of the pupil with his

higher self, is the teacher; and the problem of all problems in school management is that of securing those
qualities in the teacher which are in unity with the
best interests and highest aims of the pupil's life.

Unifying Qualities in the Teacher.

The first step in the evolution of the outer organism
is to make an objective differentiation corresponding to
the subjective one, — the teacher differentiated from the
other members of society who are to be taught. We must
not forget that education is carried on by other agencies
than those formally set apart for that purpose. The
child's touch with his environment — with nature and
with social and industrial life — has, perhaps, more influence over him than the set lessons of the teacher. This
fact saves him from the bungling work of the school-
master. The teacher may work by forced and stupefying
processes; but nature and life, by more intimate sympathy
and wiser council, and by a constant and all-sided influence, counteract conventional methods.

One is often surprised in noting how small the difference between those who have enjoyed the best school
training and those who have only intimate experience
with the world about them. This surprise comes from
not taking into account the numerous educative forces
incident to the activities of life. Said Rev. McIntyre,
"I remember the sneer of the first campaign, that Lincoln

had only got six months' education. It was wrong: it
should have been six months' schooling; he had only
that, but he was the best educated man of his time."
Shakespeare has likewise been reproached with lack of
education; and this because he "knew little Latin and
less Greek." But some one appropriately retorts that,
what was of greater moment, the Latin and Greek writers
did not know Shakespeare. It is a current remark about
people who stand out from among their fellows because
of greater power of thought, skill in using faculties, and
depth of experience, but who have had but little schooling,
that they lack education. Education does not consist in
knowing certain definite things, as Greek, Latin, or
mathematics, but in that power and versatility of thought
and emotion which elevate life into truth and virtue,
and which may come from any form of true and deep
experience which the individual has with the world
about him. Contact with the world, as well as the
tuition of the school, produces wealth of experience
and ripe wisdom. The individual's whole environment
educates him ; and the teacher, being but a small part
of this, must not be accredited nor charged with the
whole result.

But the point touching our present discussion is the
distinction between the teacher and the other educating
agencies. The other forces work incidentally, while the
teacher labors directly and exclusively to the end of
education. Nature teaches the child, but it does not
plan to do so. Citizens of the state are taught by the

state; yet teaching is not the state's direct business. The family and the church work more nearly by the direct process of instruction; yet their functions are not exclusively exercised in that direction. The church touches specifically one side of life, and this by inter-mittent process in the midst of the daily duties of those instructed. In the school, teacher and pupils both hold themselves apart to the one duty of teaching and learning. Members of the family instruct the children; but this is not their sole function, and the daily pressure of life is often so great as to prevent any systematic effort in that direction. The teacher is the one and only member of society whose sole business it is, by set plan and purpose, to develop the whole life of another. Of course he wisely leaves to the other institutions to do what they may indirectly do, — leaves the pupil to learn what the incidents of life force upon him. Why should the teacher teach the conventional ways of society, such as table manners and social etiquette, when the situations of life will more efficiently do so? Why teach a child that snow is white and cold, if he always sees snow in winter? or that one and one make two? — thus teaching what every Dodd Weaver "knowed always;" or what would be learned in due time and by natural process. Why teach a pupil to vote, while the whole structure of society is such as to give him the necessary instruction and force him to learn? Is a young man coming to voting age likely to forget the duty, when all political parties have an eye on him? and will he lack for instruction when so many well prepared are eager to give it without charging it up to the school fund? What the pupil must learn by daily contact with things should be left to the agencies of incidental instruction. Yet the teacher must take into account all the unconscious processes of the other functions of society, and make them a part of his conscious processes.

In the preceding discussion the school was shown in its deeper connection with all other institutions; it now appears different in having for its sole and direct aim the education of the individual, through an agent exclusively set apart for that purpose. It is obvious, therefore, that the first differentiating quality of the teacher is that of: —

Freedom in the Vocation. — The teacher must be able to say, "This one thing I do, and from my own highest personal interest." The first principle of school management, in external application, requires that the conditions be made such that one can well afford, from the standpoint of self-interest, to devote himself to teaching. Of course the very fact that one in so doing must withdraw from some other pursuit requires that his remuneration be equal to that in the pursuit from which he withdraws. This at once necessitates a system of raising school funds. A teacher cannot be a teacher, with salary insufficient to support himself without turning to odd jobs to meet the necessities of private and professional life. This is not simply a question of competition with other professions, but a question of professional life or death. Just in proportion as a teacher has to plough in summer in order that he may teach in winter, he is a farmer, and not a teacher. The salary must support a teacher comfortably, and enable him to keep abreast with his profession. This amount the ethics of the situation requires of every school board, whether or not it be in excess of that paid in other professions. Professional freedom must be secured.

Usually increase of teachers' salaries is urged on the ground that other professions pay better. Now a teacher cannot urge such an argument, for fear of being reminded that this is a free country, and that he should himself choose one of the lucrative vocations, or quit grumbling. Besides, the statement that other professions pay better may be questioned. While the poor pay of the teacher is proverbial, so is that of the minister and the lawyer. Think of the donation party of the one, and of the starving period of the other! From ten to twenty thousand dollar salaries are found among doctors, ministers, and lawyers; but they are also found among teachers. Teachers' salaries are, perhaps, as good as those in any other profession. But this proves nothing from the standpoint of the law of the school, which requires absolutely that the teacher be freed from the necessity of engaging in other activities while striving to follow his own vocation. He must be enabled to differentiate himself, and then required to do so.

The salary, however, is not the only personal inducement to engage in a given vocation. The question is

more properly determined by the opportunity offered
for personal culture. One should choose that vocation
which requires work as nearly as possible in the line
of his own development. The greater the divergence
between the line of one's spiritual growth and the line
of activity required in a given trade or profession, the
greater must be the salary paid, to offset the loss by
giving opportunity to make life whole in other ways than
by the labor in which one is engaged. The wood-sawyer
needs pay enough to enable him to seek other opportunities of growth than those furnished by his work; but the
teacher's activities are more nearly in the line of his own
development. Whatever be the occupation or profession,
it is incidental to the main business of life, — that of self-
realization. A teacher may, by comparison, rejoice in a
less salary than that paid to a policeman, a railroad
conductor, or a bank cashier. Who would resign a five-
hundred-dollar professorship for a thousand-dollar brakes-
manship on a freight train? No, salary is but one of
many factors securing personal freedom in the vocation of
teaching. The law of school management requires only
that the collective inducements be made sufficient to
fully differentiate the teacher from the other members of
society. The teacher, while aiding the pupil to realize
his purpose in life, must be enabled to realize his own.

But the management, after making conditions for free,
happy, and advantageous service for those qualified to
teach, must apply the law anew to secure other unifying
qualities in the teacher. While the adoption of the pro-

fession as a private good is absolutely essential, and the first resting-point in the evolution of the organism, a teacher is not a teacher by that fact alone. To decide to teach is not to become a teacher. The teacher, in serving as a means to the unity of the pupil with his ideal self, can do so only through being in unity with what the pupil is to become. Hence management must secure in the teacher: —

The Pupil's Ideal. — The unity within the pupil is secured through unity with the teacher. Unless the teacher is the better self of the pupil, he is not a teacher. Teaching, in its fundamental aspect, is not a process of going through the thought of the lesson with the pupil, but that of constant readjustment to the advancing potential self of the pupil, — to the next best possible thought, impulse, and resolution of his growing life. In the very nature of the teaching process, as shown on page 4 of "The Philosophy of Teaching" and page 17 of the present treatment, there must be identification of the teacher's life with that of the pupil. In this process the teacher is the advancing ideal of the pupil, and by the tension thus set up draws the pupil unto himself, which is also the pupil's self.

This is not true simply in a general and abstract way; for in every detail of teaching the teacher must, in the very nature of the process, adjust himself — his thought, his feeling, his life — to what the pupil ought next to become. The teacher is not merely the remote and unattainable ideal of the pupil, but, in the act of teaching, becomes the very near and present help to the next immediate good. The remote end is realized by a constant descent of the ideal into living touch with the real. Hence the teacher, to be a teacher, must be the advanced, realized ideal of the pupil. It is not sufficient for the teacher to set up imaginary ends and theories for realizing them in the pupil; he himself must be the realized end. It is scarcely worth while for a teacher to set up as an end in the pupil the formation of correct habits and forms of thought without having realized them in himself. A teacher who is not able to think with scientific patience and precision, cannot train to such patience and precision. The unifying grasp of thought can be made firm only by him who has such grasp. Truth-loving can be cultivated only by him who is a truth-lover. Strength, harmony, and beauty of character spring only from the touch of him whose character is strong, harmonious, and beautiful. The teacher's qualification is the teacher himself; and this must be taken in no remote way, and as mere example, but in the sense of intimate fusion of his life-current with that of the pupil.

This introduces a distinction which further emphasizes the law of the pupil's ideal in the teacher, — the distinction between conscious and unconscious tuition. The teacher, by conscious plan and immediate effort, by definite and formal instruction, draws the pupil into his own more perfect thought and life; but much of the influence exerted by the teacher is unconscious and without forethought, — an influence, indeed, which plan and purpose would certainly defeat. So susceptible are we to the silent influence of others that we are supposed to be permanently changed in passing another on the street. We do know, both by experience and observation, that the mysterious alchemy of influence works with marvellous power on the young who are in the continual presence of those whom they admire. Pupils instinctively copy the teacher, even to the fault of mannerisms ; from which, and all other defects of manner and life, therefore, the teacher should be free. But the pupil assimilates, as well, the beautiful traits and the wholesome spirit, which, like a fragrance, fills the air about noble-minded and warm-hearted men and women. Not so much by the fixed and hard grooves of instruction as by the silent worship of the heart does the child flower into beautiful life, and ripen into worthy manhood or womanhood. Every teacher should be to his pupil what the "Great Stone Face," in Hawthorne's story by that title, was to Ernest. When a child living in the valley among the mountains, Ernest's heart was touched by the beautiful and benign soul expressed in the "Great Stone Face." He was told of the prophecy of the coming man whom the face typified. From Ernest's childhood to his old age, renowned characters came to the valley, heralded, each in succession, as the man of prophecy; but in each case Ernest shook his head in doubt and hung it in sadness. "Will he never come?" asked Ernest, and patiently waited and worshipped in silence. Late in life he thought he had surely found the man in the poet who had arrived, and whose words Ernest had pondered. But not so; yet the poet had the insight to discern the long-sought man. Ernest, with face illumined by the setting sun and the radiance of eloquence, as he addressed his little congregation against the mountain-side, stood trans-figured by the life he had so long idealized in the "Great Stone Face." The man of prophecy was Ernest himself; he had grown to be what he had worshipped and prayed for in another.

A reformed convict, some twenty years after his release, thanked the good priest for the start given him on leaving prison. The priest asked what he had said. "Ah! it was not what you said; it was the touch." The story has it that an eaglet hatched with a brood of goslings, unconscious of its eagle nature, kept to earth with its unnatural mates, till an eagle, hovering over, swooped down upon it, and touched it into the triumphant life of the free upper air.

Thus, by the admiration and worship of a superior life, does the pupil realize the worth and beauty of that life. The closest and most precise method of instruction does not measure the teacher's responsibility. After all, the pupil may continue to walk on earth among earthly things, unless quickened by a touch from the hovering spirit in the higher life.

And so the teacher, who enters the vocation from his own interest, is permitted to do so on the condition of being the ideal life of the pupil. But he cannot be merely a passive ideal; he must actually lay hold upon the pupil. So far the approach has been made from the side of the pupil: first, by inducements to labor for him; and second, by laying hold upon the teacher's thought and life as his own ideal. Now the tension works from the other side also. Since the teacher is the pupil's other self, he should strive for the pupil as the pupil should strive for himself. This organic unity between the teacher and the pupil is the standpoint from which to answer all questions of management arising from their mutual relations. In fact, this is the standpoint for the solution of all ethical questions. All conduct should be regulated by regarding "thy neighbor as thyself." The teacher's ethics, therefore, falls under the universal law, and requires an all-absorbing enthusiasm for the child, as the high-spirited individual has for his own ideal. This disinterested devotion to the good of the pupil is known as:

Professional Spirit — 1. Professional spirit, in general, is the feeling of urgency produced by an ideal, in order that the ideal may realize itself. It is the craving for the ideal to such an extent that its realization is both the motive and the reward of the labor required to realize it. Palissy, in Longfellow's "Kéramos," is caught by the ideal of a new enamel, and works "with such good cheer;" yet his "rustic wares scarce find him bread from day to day."

> " Who is this in the suburbs here ?
>
> .   .   .   .   .
>
> This madman, as the people say,
> Who breaks his tables and his chairs
> To feed his furnace fires, nor cares
> Who goes unfed if they are fed,
> Nor who may live if they are dead ?

> This alchemist, with hollow cheeks,
> And sunken, searching eyes, who seeks,
> By mingled earths and ores combined
> With potency of fire, to find
> Some new enamel, hard and bright,
> His dream, his passion, his delight ?

> "O Palissy ! within thy breast
> Burned the hot fever of unrest;
> Thine was the prophet's vision, thine
> The exultation, the divine
> Insanity of noble minds,
> That never falters nor abates,
> But labors and endures and waits,
> Till all that it foresees it finds,
> Or what it cannot find creates."

Yes, professional spirit, in its poetic form, is "the hot fever of unrest," "the divine insanity of noble minds," laboring, enduring, and waiting to find or create what is foreseen. Labor is drudgery or joy, depending on whether the laborer is inspired by an ideal. Seeking ideals is real and true living, and only through this can life reach its full fruition. The daily routine of the hardest labor is transformed into life and delight when some ideal in the labor takes possession of the heart. When the master, in Longfellow's "Building of the Ship," received the order, —

> "Build me straight, O worthy master,
> Stanch and strong, a goodly vessel,
> That shall laugh at all disaster,
> And with wave and whirlwind wrestle," —

the poet says : —

> "The merchant's word
> Delighted the master heard ;
> For his heart was in his work, and the heart
> Giveth grace unto every art."

The master was delighted because of his opportunity to build the ideal vessel, — "a goodly vessel, that shall laugh at all disaster, and with wave and whirlwind wrestle." In this contract there was no delay, nor parleying and competitive bidding. The merchant knew well that he could trust the man whose heart was in his work, for his heart would give grace unto the art; and the master had no conditions to ask, so delighted was he at the opportunity to work out his ideal vessel. And the joy of labor was contagious; and in the long, hot days of toil, —

> " He who listened heard now and then
> The song of the master and his men:
> ' Build me straight, O worthy master,' " etc.

A skilful shoemaker, who was delighted with his labor, and who was always talking about it, when asked how it was possible to find so much pleasure in the monotonous exercise of driving pegs, replied that he tried each time to drive the peg a little "slicker." Each time he set up the ideal driving of a peg, and drove to the ideal. The old farmer who, in spite of himself, leaps the fence and the ditch to come straight to the tree that he is to fell, cannot understand the plodding motion of the hired hand, as he takes the beaten path around through the open gateway. But both move along the line of least resistance. The conditions are not such that the hired man can so easily put his heart into his work, and so he puts his time in it. How much it would aid the labor problem to secure conditions so that each laborer has an idea of his own to work out; so that it become not a question of enduring his toil, but of eager opportunity.

As much as we may say that teachers and others labor for money, yet it is also true that opportunity to realize a cherished idea is a controlling force in every healthy-minded person. There may be men who desire to be bishop, to be called bishop, as Ruskin puts it; but there are men who desire to be bishop because they see in it opportunity to work out a spiritual good in the church. There may be men who desire to be governor, just to be called governor, and for whatever adventitious gain in standing and notoriety such a position would bring; but there are men who desire to be governor to bring about a firmer administration of justice. There may be men who seek the State superintendency because of the distinction attending such a noble office; but there are men who could feel no such elevation, because possessed by educational doctrine and conviction, which sweep away petty and ignoble considerations. There may be teachers whose motive is the pay, and pride of position; but there are teachers who seek labor because they feel that they can secure an educational result which is impersonal and disinterested; they feel a potency for good in them, and crave most of all an opportunity to realize it. It is useless to ask whether a teacher labor for salary; it is only proper to ask whether he labor for a disinterested good while supported by his salary. An increase of salary does not lessen professional interest, but rather increases it, by freeing the teacher from the anxiety of self-support.

The more salary the teacher gets, the less does he need to work for it; the less his professional spirit is starved by foreign considerations.   Yet external conditions cannot quench or modify much the genuine professional spirit. It will "burn with the hot fever of unrest."

The true professional spirit of the teacher develops through two lower phases.   In the lowest phase the teacher has the heart set on skilful manipulation of school machinery, — the perfect way of moving classes, calling the roll, asking questions, manipulating devices ornamenting school-room, — in short, the perfect military and material side of the school.   This is a worthy, but not the highest, phase of professional spirit.

The next phase in the ascending order of professional spirit is that in which the teacher's interest lies in the skilful manipulation of mental processes in the art of learning.   His ideal is the perfect movement of the child's mind through a given bit of subject-matter.   It does not include the sum total of the educative processes, but only the subject-matter dealt with in individual recitations, or in given portions of subject-matter, — as the multiplication of one fraction by another, the raising of cotton, or the "Song of Hiawatha."   All this is a worthy ideal, and the immediate end for which the perfect mechanics of the school exist, as sought by the ideal of the preceding phase.

The highest phase of professional spirit has its ideal in the development of the child as an entire process.   All the individual lessons are held in the unity of the ideal unfolding of the child's life.   Each lesson is now seen, not only in its individual nature, but in its final issue. The perfect being toward which the child moves is the conscious principle, guiding the concrete work of lesson-hearing, and also the lower phase of external manipulation.   An individual lesson may be very skilful and beautiful, when considered merely in itself, but found blundering and deformed when examined in light of the final good.   The passion of the teacher must be for the ultimate good of the child, and not the immediate seeming good.   The feeling which arises from teaching with a consciousness of the ultimate good is the highest possible phase of professional spirit.   It is much more difficult to attain to than either of the preceding, and but comparatively few reach it, — perhaps difficult because it is the highest generalization of all the educative forces.   Enthusiasm for the child, and not for machinery and pretty lesson processes, regulated by consciousness of the rational process of educating him, is truly professional spirit. This is the point at which the teacher reaches "the divine insanity of noble minds."   Palissy attained it working in clay.   Why can't we, working in life?

The great teachers who have come down to us through history are so because of their devotion, yea, their un-bounded enthusiasm, for the pupil.   Can we doubt it after reading the life of Pestalozzi, Froebel, Arnold, Horace Mann, Mark Hopkins?   The theorist and the philosopher may make their mark as such, but the man or woman known, esteemed, honored, and loved as a teacher, must become so through intense sympathy with the unfolding life of others, — a sympathy which gives no peace except in the self-forgetful labor of nurturing the life of those struggling for better things.

The requirement of professional spirit, by which the teacher forgets himself in the pupil, is not in conflict with the requirement of freedom in the profession, by which the teacher serves from personal interest. Rather they are in perfect harmony, — in fact, organic unity, for man cannot find his life except by losing it. His subjective processes of growth must be absorbed in some objective product felt to be good on its own account. Those attaining the highest excellence are not self-seekers. Man cannot grow in charity by thinking of his growth in charity. Patriotism flourishes best in him who is too busy in his country's service to think of his patriotism. When Wilberforce was heroically devoting his life to freeing the slaves in the West Indies, he was reminded by a good Christian lady that he was neglecting religion and the welfare of his soul. He replied that he was too busy to know that he had a soul. Think you that he was not saving it? There is no way to attain to moral sublimity except by tension with a universal, objective good, which obliterates self-consciousness in the seeking. The same law holds whether in the moral or intellectual life; no personal height can be attained by thinking on the self as attaining it. Self-sacrifice is the law of self-realization; but this is not the passive yielding up of life, rather the highest form of self-assertion. Hence the teacher, from the highest standpoint of self-interest, must forget himself in his zeal to save his pupil.

It seems much easier for the kindergarten teacher to obey this law than for the professor in the university. The latter does indeed lose himself, but too often in his subject instead of his student. The modern university, with its intense spirit of research, is an opportunity for distinction in scholarship, and original production of learned theses. This clearly divides the faculty into two functions, — that of teacher and student; but the law still holds that a teacher is a teacher only in devoting himself to the student. Of course the professor is of more value to the student in being a living, growing man himself; but there is a temptation, too strong for some to bear, of leaving the student out of the account altogether. The absorption in his line of investigation, and lack of interest in the personal welfare of his students, seems to be the spirit of the modern university professor. The student sometimes puts it as "lack of soul;" but this feeling may arise from an unnatural craving for attention on the part of the student, and a failure to make allowance for the fact that the requirements of the subject grow more rigid, and those of the student for direct help less so, on reaching the university phase of school work. In the kindergarten the subject taught is easily managed, so far as the knowledge required is concerned; but the pupil here must have immediate, constant, and sympathetic attention. In either case the teacher is a teacher, and a great teacher, just in proportion as he, by generous sympathy, compasses, inspires, and guides the life intrusted to his care; and no more than the kindergarten teacher can the university professor escape the law. Yet we read in the "Educational Review" for January, 1895, on "Necessary Reforms in the Colleges," that: —

"In the zeal for special research which . . . has become the ideal aim of much college instruction, it has come about that only the most brilliant scholars are chosen to be instructors, regardless of their lack of more strictly professional preparation and experience. . . . ' These men, generally students of high standing, who, after graduation, have seen something of German universities, cannot conceive their function as did the worthy teacher of a hundred years ago. . . . Some teachers of the old school naturally remain, — teachers in whom the moral and personal relation to their pupils is still predominant; but the main concern of our typical young professor is not his pupils at all. It is his science. . . . But, generally speaking, he wishes to be a scholar, and is a teacher only by accident, — only because scholars are as yet supported by institutions whose primary object is the education of youth. . . .' [1]

"The attitude of professors of the type Dr. Santayana has described, toward associates of what I deem a better type, is very clearly disclosed by such remarks as the following. A prominent professor in one of the foremost American colleges, speaking of a distinguished colleague

---

[1] Quoted by the writer from Dr. George Santayana on the spirit and ideals of one of our celebrated American Universities.

recently, said to an acquaintance, ' Oh, he 's nothing but a teacher!' Under similar circumstances, a professor in another well-known college was overheard to use nearly the same language, referring to a colleague whose name is almost a household word among teachers and scholars: ' He 's a mere teacher.' So far had these eminent gentlemen adopted the view that scholarship and enthusiasm for research are the supreme essentials to success and superiority as professors, that they could employ the unwarranted assumption not only without attempt at proof, but in terms of sincere contempt for eminent colleagues. Could the speakers know the frequent comparisons, highly unfavorable to themselves, made by some of the best students of their respective colleges between them and the colleagues they tried to belittle, they might be greatly surprised and chagrined."

2. But professional spirit is much more than a susceptibility and eagerness to respond to the pupil's need, — more than blind enthusiasms for what the pupil's life holds in prophecy. In addition, there must be consciousness of skill in aiding the pupil to realize the highest ideal of human life. The teacher must feel confident, through a knowledge of the nature and laws of spiritual growth, of safe and certain guidance to the end sought. Professional spirit is thus a sense of the power to accomplish an end by a rational process, — a process by which every step in detail is felt in relation to the ultimate end. The teacher must rise above the consciousness of the external means, and of the mental processes involved in

teaching a particular lesson, to the consciousness of the universal value to the child of every teaching act. A teacher may be conscious of the external means by which to teach a cube to a child, and may have analyzed the process by which he forms his concept cube; but unless he can state and feel the value of the cube-experience in terms of the pupil's unfolding life, he has no intelligent reason for, and no professional spirit in, producing the experience. He may know the material means and mental process by which the pupil forms his picture of the earth, but he can have no reason for causing its formation, and cannot rationally and with professional spirit do so, unless he knows how such a process and product is to aid the pupil in the solution of life's problem.

Every lesson the teacher hears alters in some way, and permanently, the pupil's whole after life. A pebble dropped in the Atlantic disturbs all its waters, the waters of the Pacific, the solid parts of the earth, the air above, and through these the cosmic forces of the universe. Every lesson re-shapes the pupil's entire life; gives it new motion, new current, new tendencies, and, through the wonderful alchemy of influences, it modifies the spiritual forces of the world. Ordinarily, the teacher's consciousness does not go beyond the here and the now of the lesson. Yet every time the pupil's life is touched, the waves circle out to the other shore, and the teacher should keep his eye on the other shore. The teacher must never be satisfied, and never can be professional in the highest sense, until he becomes conscious of the ultimate end in the process of its realization. And this must be taken in no abstract and general sense; it means that this teacher, here and now, in this particular First Reader lesson, is vividly conscious of its full life-meaning in the act of conducting the lesson. In general propositions we admit all this; but what needs to be insisted on is the necessity that the teacher in his daily, concrete teaching experience, be stimulated and guided by the largest meaning which the lesson has for the child. All this is but an aspect of the law of unity; for this law requires the teacher to keep himself in unity with the future self of the pupil, in order that the pupil may reach that self.

Fusing now the first and second elements of professional spirit, we have the consciousness of realizing ideals by rational procedure, — procedure through organized steps to a clearly defined end.

3. If we draw more completely under the law of unity, we shall find professional spirit to be a still fuller experience than yet indicated. The self which the pupil is to become, and with which the teacher must be identified, is the thought and spirit of the world objective to the pupil. The teacher must compass in his own life the organic unity of the pupil and the outer world ; stated in a superficial way as knowledge of the pupil and of the subject-matter. But this must be a knowledge of the two as one; for the pupil — this self to be taught — includes science, literature, history, etc., either really or potentially. These are his present, and are to be his future, experiences, connected by one whole of life activity. The

teacher is the connecting instrument between the old experience and the new, having brought both into terms of his own life.

The branches to be taught are only processes of thought or forms of experience by which the pupil finds his life in the infinite life about him. Therefore, when it is said that the teacher must be the other self to the pupil, it is implied that this objective world to the pupil is already made the teacher's own. He must know from experience the relation of the thought and spirit of the world to the growing life of his pupil. The little flower has whispered to him of the infinite, and he must know what message it has to his blindly craving pupil. The lily has spoken to him its thought, plan, and purpose; its innocence, purity, and beauty; and he feels by sympathy how much the more limited life of his pupil needs such experiences. He has felt the strength, self-sacrifice, and heroism of Socrates, and knowing that his pupil must grow in firmness of virtue, brings Socrates' life into the pupil's experience. The teacher must see to it that the heavens declare the glory of God to the pupil, but they must first have declared it to the teacher. Thus the soul of the objective world is transformed into the life of the pupil through the experience of the teacher.

Professional spirit thus involves a consciousness of subject-matter as connected experience in the process of spiritual growth. It cannot be urged too often that a teacher must know his subject in and of itself; that he cannot teach what he does not know; and that he cannot teach even what he does teach without knowing vastly more than the pupil is expected to learn. The wealth of experience one has had in a subject is the largest determining factor in his professional preparation, for this experience is the spiritual medium by which the pupil comes into unity with the life of the objective world, which is his larger self. But we often hear that knowledge of subject-matter alone is not sufficient; that there must be knowledge of methods of instruction. The sharp opposition usually drawn between these two seems to be unfortunate; yet it will serve to enforce the truth. In a convention of teachers, some of whom are trained in the normal school and some in the college, we expect to hear from one side the imputation of a lack of professional training, and from the other the sneer at method in an empty head; because, perhaps, both are somewhat empty, — one in not seeing that the subject has the method within itself, and the other in failing to note that method must find itself in the subject; it cannot dangle in the air. Whatever it may be called, the teacher must see his subject as an unfolding experience in the life of the pupil, and not simply as a system of thought having its own logical coherence. Knowledge of subject-matter is a system of thought, organized about some central principle announced by the subject-matter itself; but the teacher must organize the subject-matter about the life of the pupil; it is means now to the child as end. It is not a question of logical coherence wholly, but also of chronological experience in the learner. At any rate, the subject, in the most fundamental view, is a mental process, rather than a product; and a process has method. A consciousness of the process of a subject in becoming the realized self of the learner is, by the law of unity, an essential element in professional spirit.

This last requirement, more than any other, puts the greatest strain upon the teacher; and is therefore the highest test of professional preparation. It not only requires a knowledge of the psychology of the learner, and of the logic of the subjects by which he is taught, but of the unity of the two in an educative process. This process is bewilderingly complex, because of the many-sidedness of the learner's life, and of the world which administers to the interests of that life; and this if life is considered only by cross section, but much more when viewed in its on-going, with new needs, interests, and aspirations at every turn. This introduces the most complex and baffling conception with which the teacher has to deal, — the Course of Study. This is made up of co-existent (practically) and successive experiences with the objective world of thought as formulated in the branches of the school course. The needs of child life at any one period can be satisfied only by touching the most diverse lines and phases of subject-matter; and with every stage of progress these assume new divisions and varied aspects. What lines of work fuse most naturally and helpfully into a present life experience, and what phases of each follow in a natural order of growth, is the greatest of all problems for the teacher. The emphasis given to this problem at present is a hopeful sign. "Correlation" and "sequence of studies" are capital words in the teacher's vocabulary; especially so if not taken to mean the stiff and formal program of parallel columns, with yearly cross sections for mere convenience of school machinery; but in the true and inward sense of variety, unity, and volume of experience, moving by steady progress to full-orbed manhood and womanhood. A course of study is a statement of the process of self-realization in terms of subject-matter; it is growing subjective experience put in objective form, determined not by logic but by the interests and necessities of life.

For practical purposes the whole course of study must be worked out in quite minute details. No matter if a teacher teach but a single grade, that work cannot be done intelligently without a sense of its organic relation to the whole. Nothing is more fatal to professional spirit than for a teacher in a graded school to passively accept a course planned by the superintendent. The teacher must feel himself to be in harmony with the whole course, which requires a sense of the whole; besides, the harmony and rhythm of the whole course requires intelligent adjustment to the whole by each who conducts a part. Such a detailed statement as required cannot here be even sketched, for this would require a special treatise on a course of study. Nothing further can here be done than to emphasize the necessity of a clear conception of such a course on the part of every teacher. The underlying principles I have tried to present on pages 246–260 in "The Philosophy of Teaching."

And thus professional spirit has grown to be conscious-ness of the unfolding life of the learner in forms and processes of subject-matter.

4. Having brought the teacher into this elevation of professional life, it seems at first that nothing more could be desired. But it will be remembered from the first chapter that the teacher comes into unity with the pupil through the elaborate machinery of the school organization. Much of this at best he has to wield as a means to the teaching process. If his care be limited to his own school-room, there is much of manipulation indirectly related to the teaching act; the teacher must bring all the conditions and forces into the central process above described. And this requires that, along with his own sense of immediate unity with the life of the pupil, there be sensitiveness to the unity of the whole organism which conditions his success in the act of instruction.

Lack of sensitiveness to the unity of the organism is the chief source of failure in school management. The teacher who does not at all times feel that the school is a whole with focused energy, will necessarily permit the dissolution of the organism. If, for instance, the sense of unity is so obtuse as not to be disturbed by the young lady who does fancy needlework in the recitation, or as to permit the teacher to pass to the back of the room to engage in a private conversation with a pupil, nothing is to be expected but disorder and confusion throughout.

This sensitiveness to unity arises from the form and habit of organic thought, — of grasping diversity into unity.

It requires a great stress of conception to hold into unity such a complex object and process as the school. What the teacher needs is a severe course of mental training to grasp complex functions into a single process. This training is not peculiar to school management, but is secured by the proper form of thinking any subject. To think rigidly the human body as an organism secures the proper habit and form of thought for grasping the school as an organism. To see all the parts in the great panorama of history as co-operating to the single issue of a great principle is to prepare the mind for the complex conception which is the basis of practical school management. Any discussion of school management which yields only a loose aggregate of topics and rules counteracts in habit of thought more than it contributes by its generous supply of precepts. All this suggests the important principle that a teacher must not have too much faith in immediate, short, and direct processes of preparation; but must know that whatever trains the mind to its perfect work gives the needed special preparation for any situation and duty of school life; that there is no way to prepare himself, or his pupils either, for practical duties, but to train himself to fundamental forms and habits of thought and life. Hence the teacher who would bring his school into unity and harmony of process must come to the work with a keen sense of unity and harmony, grounded in thorough training in organic forms and habits of thought. To make the school in form of unity, the teacher must first have reduced himself to that form,—

into an abiding consciousness of unity in presence of the school organism. This is the final element sought in professional spirit.

Professional consciousness has now grown to be quite complex and organic. First, there appeared the self-forgetful sympathy and enthusiasm for the pupil in the general interests and aspirations of his life; second, the pupil's ideal was clearly grasped in the process of its unfolding, giving rise to a definite sense of the process of self-realization; third, the objective world appeared in organic relation to the subjective process, giving rise to the consciousness of organic unity between the subjective and the objective self; and fourth, there arose the consciousness of the unity of the external organism with the process of unity between teacher and pupil. These are the elements of professional spirit in the order of evolution, under the force of the law of unity discovered in the first chapter; and, taken altogether, form the attribute in the individual denoted by the word teacher. These elements, therefore, in their organic order, suggest a definite scheme for the examination of the teacher. It is not proper here to make out in detail the questions and directions for such a test, but it might be well for the reader to do so; and, after comparing with those currently used, imagine the result in substituting the new for the old. We hesitate and falter before such ideals; yet the only manly and helpful thing to do is to face them fairly and hopefully. We may not reach our highest ideals, certainly not the ideal of ideals, which would be God Himself; but there is no high and worthy effort except in faith of the ultimate reality of ideals. Falter before them we may, but we cannot escape living and acting under them.

UNIFYING CONDITIONS OF TEACHER AND PUPILS.

Let it be constantly held that the primary unity sought is that between the pupil's real and ideal self; that every teaching act should bring the pupil into unity with his next best self. By this unity as a standard, the qualities of the teacher have been outlined in the preceding chapter. But that these qualities may be effective, the teacher must come into living touch with the pupil. We are now concerned, therefore, with the conditions of unity between teacher and pupils, — a secondary unity as a means to the primary.

The unifying qualities in the teacher needed development, but the unifying qualities in the pupil must be assumed as the basis of the whole process. The school arises out of the impulse of the student to unity with his higher life, and hence his impulse to unity with his teacher. We must admit, as a basis of the school process, the fact that the pupil is naturally inclined to learn, and to join with one who will guide him. This is the fundamental premise in the argument that a school is defective when pupils are adverse to attendance. If the school-house is a house of life, and learning a process of living, how can school work be repulsive, except on the assumption that it is antagonistic to the interests of life. If the pupil must think of the school as a task and imprisonment, instead of joyous, free life, something must be wrong with the school rather than with the pupil. Barring the question of perverted habits and tastes, the teacher can have no higher criterion for his work than the joyous and eager school-going which results from his instruction. Since the school arises from the student's impulse of growth, and is a process of that growth, his own consciousness of growth, with the accompanying satisfaction, must be the ultimate standard of testing efficiency. If students cease to elect the work of a professor, this evidence ought to convince the president of the professor's inefficiency; and if all professors were thus abandoned, it would be attributed to worthlessness of the institution, rather than stubborn perversity in the students. The student's desire to go to school, when the conditions of true living are supplied, is the ultimate fact and test of school work. A compulsory school law is compulsory to parents rather than to pupils; it is to protect the pupil against the invasion of his rights by parents and others. This law is an enactment by the needs of the pupil's own life, and sanctioned by his more developed reason as embodied in others; it is nothing more than a legalized expression of the student's school-going desire.

In the case of the teacher it is found necessary to offer inducements to enter the vocation; but the very nature of the pupil's life craves being taught; so much so, that he pays for the opportunity of co-operating with the teacher in forming the school. Hence we cannot speak of securing qualites of unity in the pupil, as was necessary in the case of the teacher, but only of the pupil's conditions of unity. The pupil demands, besides certain qualities in the teacher, the conditions by which he may enter into concrete and living unity with the teacher. Whatever his qualifications, the teacher standing apart is of no service to the pupil. The first and most general condition is that which secures: —

Personal Contact. — Teaching cannot be carried on in absence of the pupil, although a faint attempt is sometimes made through correspondence. Since the pupil is to enjoy the general elevating influence of the teacher, he must be brought within the atmosphere of the teacher. Personal touch is absolutely essential to the influence of the life-giving principle. The teacher, as the unconscious ideal of the pupil, has no power in the absence of the pupil; the radius of the charmed circle is measured by the distinct intonations of the voice, the sparkle of the eye, and the beaming of the soul in the countenance.

And the same condition is no less rigidly required by direct instruction. Such, when possible by correspondence, lacks vivacity, flexibility, and power. Except in the living presence of the pupil, the teacher cannot adjust himself to the varying moods and unexpected movements of the mind in the process of learning. Especially exacting is this law in teaching children. On account of the child's inability to hold a continuous line of thought, the process of teaching would be instantly obstructed by its withdrawal from the school-room. The longer a pupil can hold himself to a proposed line of investigation, the more may he free himself from the presence of the teacher; and complete freedom is gained on condition of complete self-control. This law is clearly marked in practice; for while the primary pupil does his work wholly in the presence of the teacher, the university student works most in his absence, hoping soon to discharge him altogether. By teaching, then, we are to understand the immediate, direct, face-to-face stimulus of one mind on another. The fact already announced, that in teaching the two minds move as one, requires personal contact.

Hence the first step in operating the external machinery is to bring pupils and teacher together at a given time and place. The law of obedience to the requirement of time and place derives its authority from the fact that without this particular form of obedience the co-opera-tion of teacher and pupil is impossible. The law against absence and tardiness does not derive its validity from the school board or the legislature, but from the nature of teaching. Truancy is wrong because it renders impos-sible the oneness of mind between teacher and pupil necessary to instruction. The pupil or the teacher who is wilfully tardy or absent, does that which, if done by all who have the same right, would completely destroy the school organization, because it blocks the machinery at the working-point. And the same right is extended to all by the law breaker, from the fact that he assumes such privilege. Thus the tax-payer and child are robbed by the mere fact of absence or tardiness. This requirement of time and place is sacred, and teacher and pupils should feel under the strictest obligations to keep it inviolate. There should be the most rigid adherence to exact time in opening and closing the day and its sessions. The ethical value of such obedience is to be discussed under the general heading of ethical value of school management. I speak here only of such obedience in relation to the organic unity of teacher and pupil in the act of instruction; in relation, therefore, to the organic unity of the whole system.

This law of personal contact determines the size of the class or school to be put in charge of a single teacher. That individual needs may be satisfied, there must be opportunity for intimate personal acquaintance. The more helpless the student, the smaller must be the classes and the school; although in practice this is usually reversed, crowding more of smaller than of larger pupils in a given space. So much depends on general conditions, especially in the training and power of the student, that no definite statement can be made as to the proper number. A primary teacher does well to manage a class of ten or a school of twenty; while in the upper grades management ought to be no more difficult, so far as the number is concerned, with classes of twenty and a school of forty. When the conditions are definitely known, the principle which requires the closest personal influence and necessary individual assistance, is the sufficient guide in practice.

This law of personal contact in teaching requires the school-room, with its appointments as a mere dwelling-place. Thus there arises out of the preceding a second external condition of unity; namely: —

The School-room. — Considered as a place of residence, the school-room must be made a positive influence in securing unity between teacher and pupil. It must be more than a secure, quiet, and comfortable meeting-place for teacher and pupil; it must have a positively elevating influence, bringing the pupil, by its active toning power, into the higher life and mood of unity with the teacher. The pupil comes at once under the combined influence of the presence of the teacher and the more indefinable presence of the school-room.

The school-room must be homelike and cheerful, pleasing and attractive. It should not be bare, hard, and repulsive, but filled with sunshine and delight. which makes it more attractive and cheering than the home of the average child. This does not require up-holstered furniture and elaborate decorations. Clean walls, with here and there a well-chosen picture, which can speak to the mind and heart of the child; neat window-curtains; a few flowers; some carpeting, — the more the better; and whatever little matters good taste would suggest. The tone of the school-room, aside from inducing the mood of mind favorable to unity of thought, is one of the powerful unconscious influences shaping the character of the child, and should receive as careful attention as the multiplication table. Court-houses are often quite expensively carpeted, to be bespattered by coarse men whose formative period is passed; while school-houses have bare walls, floors, and platforms, to be occupied the whole day by pure, susceptible childhood. A more refining power in the school-room, and the court-room becomes the less useful. The court-house is not over done; the school-house is under done. The teacher must not wait for the trustee or director to do expensive things; with no expense, except the free contribution of pupils, in articles and in labor, the school-room can be made quite cheery. The will finds the way.

The general relation of presence of teacher and pupil in a properly toned school-room must now assume definite: —

Communicable Relation of Teacher and Pupils. — The immediate condition of unity is that which makes possible the exchange of thought through speech, look, and gesture. Hence, securing communicable relation, to the end of unity in the act of instruction, requires more than the mere presence of teacher and pupils in the school-room at a given time. Teacher and pupils must be brought face to face as in the act of communication. This requires pupils to be seated in a compact form, so that the teacher can seize the entire group in one view; and so that each pupil in the group is in easy conversational relation with the teacher. The seated portion of the room should not be so wide from right to left, or so long from front to back, that all the pupils cannot be equally distinctly addressed by eye and voice. If classes are to be heard in their seats, say in the left, middle, or right of the room the width of the room from right to left would be increased by what it should be for convenience in grasping the school as a whole. In such a case there should be a compromise between the two requirements. If the school is to be addressed always as a whole, as often the case in a high school, the seated portion should be about square; if two grades are to be in the room, the seated portion should be about one third wider from right to left than from front to back. The audience room of a modern church, with its settees circled about the pulpit as a centre, and elevated in the rear, is a recognition of the principle here to be enforced.

It is not well to have the body of the school separated by stoves or wide aisles; the external form of unity should be maintained. The rows of desks should be placed with perfect regularity, and the whole should be made to look well as a body. When there are only a few pupils for the number of desks, these pupils should not be scattered so as to give the whole a ragged appearance. Compactness and external form of unity furthers the mental unity sought. It is wise foresight to visit the school-room before opening school, and make sure that the seating is in proper form.

This law of seating so as to secure easy communicable relations, requires the teacher to keep himself in front of the pupils. He should not, for instance, go to the back of the room to aid a pupil; he should be where he can see and be seen, hear and be heard. Not that he may watch for mischief, but that he be always in convenient position for communication, — that he may constantly grasp the whole in unity, and avoid the school's falling to pieces by breaking the lines of unity between himself and each individual pupil.

Teacher and pupil being now placed in definite position of unity with reference to each other, a further necessity arises, which must be met by adjustment of external conditions. The foregoing conditions confine and constrain both teacher and pupils, and consume energy which should be expended on the teaching and the learning act. Thus arises the third problem touching external conditions, that of : —

Economy of Energy in Teacher and Pupils. — Teacher and pupils have but a given amount of energy for the work in hand; and the amount wasted because of unfavorable conditions incident to school-room confinement is so much subtracted from unity in the teaching process. The law of unity requires all the mental energy of the teacher and the pupil expended on the subject under consideration. Therefore, the conditions must be such as not to divert a portion of their energy to something aside from the line of discussion. The school-room conditions necessarily divert some energy from the effort for which the school-room exists, just as a part of the force generated for a given purpose by a machine is destroyed by the machine itself. This friction must be reduced to the minimum ; and to do so the ways in which energy is wasted must be ascertained. Of these there can be but two: (1) uncomfortable bodily condition may divert the attention to self; or (2) attention may be diverted to some other object aside from the line of discussion.

1. The physical condition of teacher and pupil must be such that they are not conscious of themselves; or, better, such that their mental energy will be intensified by physical vigor. The conditions cannot supply red blood, or prompt the rhythmical pulse, but much can be done by way of conserving energy and securing comfort to the body while in the school-room. And for himself, while out of school, the teacher must guard his physical condition, and keep in good trim for the school-room. The law of the school forbids late hours and dissipation, and enjoins the utmost care in preserving the physical and mental vigor for the strain of teaching and managing. While in the school-room, the teacher must avoid undue exertion, — must sit when at all convenient, and avoid vexation and worry. The teacher should be relieved of the unjust burden of reports usually imposed, and the work of teacher's meetings made as light as possible. The exaction of boards and superintendents in reports from teachers, by way of keeping the system well articulated, often tends strongly toward the dissolution of the organism altogether, in diverting the energy of the teacher from the vital point of the organism.

Under the first point of economizing energy, the following specific conditions must be secured: —

a. Seats should be so comfortable that the body is kept rested, — should be the shape of the body, and neither too high nor too low. Much is properly said on hygienic grounds against the high desk for small pupils; but I wish here to emphasize the fact that such is also detrimental to the act of instruction. The old split puncheon seat without back was very uncomfortable, and thus very much opposed to mental unity of teacher and pupil. We find here also the grounds for intermissions and for frequent physical exercises. The pupil must be kept rested and invigorated, not only as a matter of preserving health, but of securing undivided attention.

b. The air should be kept at the proper temperature. If a pupil is chilled, his attention is directed to himself; and in a room of forty chilled pupils there are forty unities instead of one. It would be difficult to over-estimate the waste from inefficient heating apparatus. With a small stove in one corner of a large room on a cold day, unity is impossible, and the day wasted. The air must be kept at a uniform and a proper temperature all over the room, or the efficiency of the teaching act is impaired, — impaired just in that proportion in which the attention is directed to the self.

c. The effect of bad ventilation on the mental activity is obvious. Drowsiness and depression weaken and divert mental energy, and prevent the fullest co-operation of thought in the line of discussion. Hence the teaching act, as well as health, requires a perfect system of ventilation, and the care of the teacher as to the constant supply of pure air in the school-room.

d. Since the process of unity is partly carried on through reading and writing, the lighting of the room must be such that no effort is required through the sense of sight. Just in proportion as seeing becomes difficult or painful, is the teaching act obstructed, as well as the eye injured. This means that there must be sufficient light, and from the proper direction.

Thus all these points, — seating, heating, ventilating, and lighting, — so properly urged as matters of health, are the conditions to receive attention in securing unity in the act of instruction; for bad seating, heating, ventilating, and lighting make the body so uncomfortable that the pupil necessarily thinks of himself instead of the subject being treated. These, and all other points in the external conditions which divert the attention from the topic under consideration to the self, must receive careful attention; and this not only in a negative way, for these conditions should be made to stimulate the energy required in teaching and learning. To remove obstruction is not sufficient; the light, and the air, and the restful position must exhilarate the mind, and urge the unity which they negatively condition.

2. If the attention is not diverted from the lesson to the self, it may still be attracted to some other object aside from the line of thought. This may be occasioned through one of the senses, especially through touch, sight, or hearing; or by some preceding train of the thought in which the mind is absorbed.

a. Because objects which the pupil or teacher may touch are apt to attract attention, all objects, other than those required in the immediate work, should be removed from the desk. Let there be an apple, a ball, a knife, or a pen on the desk, and it seems almost impossible for the pupil to refrain from handling it; and thus having other thoughts awakened than those desired. The advantage of single over double desks arises at this point. Every experienced teacher knows how much less is the strain to keep order with pupils seated single than when seated double, — so much less that it is wise economy for the trustee to buy the single desk at a much greater cost.

b. Since attention is apt to be attracted through the eye, all unnecessary movement about the room should be avoided, and all the objects in the room be orderly bestowed. Pupils passing in and out during school sessions; getting drink; coal bucket out of place; one curtain down and another up, etc., etc., — all confuse the attention through the eye.

c. Most effective of all means of diverting the attention is that of noise. Silence must be the law of the school-room. The noise of whispering, studying, fixing fires, walking, loud talk of teacher, etc., must be gotten rid of. It is quite common for the teacher to make more noise than all the pupils together. A teacher should speak in subdued tones, and move about too quietly to attract notice. He should so address a class during recitation that the pupils studying are not compelled to listen. Pencils should be sharpened at recess; and slate frames covered, or slates abolished for note-books.

I know it has been often urged that a noisy school-room is a sign of energy and activity, of industry and hard work; that the working beehive must hum. This sounds very well till we reflect that it is physical energy and activity that makes the noise; there is no mental analogy. Rather it is the reverse; for the greater the mental activity the greater the silence. The boy who thinks is not necessarily noisy, but necessarily silent. All professional students seek a silent retreat as the best condition for mental labor. This doctrine of a noisy school arises from two classes of teachers, — those who cannot secure silence, and seek an escape through the theory; and those who champion in good faith the plea for freedom on the part of the pupil, — or, as it seems to some, a plea for license.

d. Little can be said to free the mind from prepossessing moods and trains of thought. The opening exercises have a value at this point. Pupils gather in the schoolroom in the morning, bringing with them their diverse interests and thoughts born of their multifarious duties, amusements, and associations. The opening exercise draws their minds to a centre; the music brings them into a common mood; and the Scripture lesson recalls them from their ramblings, and tones the thought for the labor of the day. I believe that opening exercises are justified on the score of school management, as well as on account of religious culture.

Having now brought teacher and pupils into the tonic atmosphere of the school-room, and having secured definite communicable relations in face-to-face position; and further, having made the conditions such as not to divert

energy from the self to other objects, but rather such as
to stimulate energy in the direction desired, teacher and
pupils must now be supplied with: —

Instruments of School Work. — At first the school-house
appears as a convenient, comfortable, and homelike abode;
and second, with such added furniture and arrangement
as necessary to bring teacher and pupils into definite relation for the interchange of thought.   Certain appliances
must yet be added to complete the outfit of every well-
furnished school-house.   These are blackboards, with
accompanying instruments; maps, charts, and devices for
illustrating subjects; laboratories, library, and text-books.

The blackboard is the constant means by which the
teacher and pupils exchange thoughts through demonstration, outline, and graphic illustration.   Maps, charts,
and illustrative devices, as globes and mathematical
forms, are the more perfect and fixed forms of communication; while the work on the blackboard, though
more crude, is the more pliable and more immediate to
the teacher's necessities.

The laboratory differs from the foregoing in not being
graphic and illustrative, but in providing for the manipulation of the actual material studied.   It is a means for
multiplying the powers of observation; both by way of
supplying material for observation, and also through
instruments which multiply the powers of the senses;
with others which alter the conditions of the object to be
observed.   Laboratories are quite a conspicuous part of
a college or university outfit; but high schools are just

beginning to realize their value, and to supply themselves accordingly. Their indispensable service to grammar and primary grades is yet to be recognized. The teacher in the primary school who values truly the study of nature must feel hindered in a school without some chemical and physical appliances. The laboratory, or at least some means of experimental study, has not been called for more earnestly because the study of nature so far has been forced in the back-ground by the more conventional studies. When observation and experimental studies assume their proper place in primary and elementary education, then the laboratory will be a prominent part of the common-school cutfit. The child's education begins in the great laboratory of nature, and his studies should be continued unbroken, but in a more rigid and systematic way, He must be trained to observe more accurately and thoroughly, and by the use of instruments to persuade nature to reveal the mysteries which she will not voluntarily disclose.

The necessity of a library is better understood; but in this, too, we find the same decreasing importance attached in descending to primary instruction. It would be difficult to state how largely a university in these days consists in a library. Class-room work is reduced to a minimum, students spending their time in the library investigating subjects under the direction of the teacher. As in the case of laboratories, high schools are beginning to understand the value and use of libraries, and the library is gradually taking its place in every well-regulated high school. When teachers in the lower grades understand the science and the art of teaching, and thus gain freedom from the conventional school drill for definite, ponderable products in the dogmatic form of text-books, the library will be as much demanded there as in the university. Of course the organization of such a library and the use of the books will be different. For instance, multiple copies of the same book would be needed, so that the teacher could use it with the class as a whole. Instead of the regulation reader, the teacher who did not work by the page would be truly happy to have in the library copies enough of Hawthorne's "Tanglewood Tales" to supply his fourth grade, and in a few weeks be able to substitute Whittier's Poems, etc. The child in the primary grade has the right to a supply of the best juvenile literature. Are not nature, history, and mythological stories as necessary to the child's culture as science, history, and philosophy are to the university student? And if so, is it not the business of the school, as much in one case as in the other, to supply the necessary books? Forces are already moving strongly to the formation of libraries for primary and grammar grades. Never before was there so much stir about young people's literature, and through agencies at work many common schools now have a nucleus of a library. When the conviction comes that a library is an essential part of the outfit of every school, then the library will come as a matter of course, as does the school-house and blackboard. And when it does come, it will do more than all other agencies to infuse with fuller and richer life the hard pedantic drill of the school-master.

With all that has been said against text-books, they are still essential instruments of school work. The library may supplant some, and render others less necessary, but its main effect on text-books will be that of forcing to their intelligent use. We cannot refuse all things which are abused. The abuse of the text by following it so slavishly as to make the pupil feel that the form and compass of knowledge are bound therein, cannot be too strongly condemned. But the text-book, used as a convenient guide to the discussion, and re-enforced by wide reading in reference books, must ever remain an efficient means of instruction.

Unifying Qualities and Conditions Secured.

Efficient co-operation, involved in the process of instruction, requires a teacher having the qualities already named to face the pupils under the conditions specified. Such is the condition of instruction demanded by the nature and need of the pupil. Yet this is not usually a conscious demand on his part. But his unconscious need gives law to the school with as much authority as though he advocate his own wants in logical form; yet public sentiment must voice his needs for him. All that has been outlined must be in the thought of the public, and brought into reality by some agency beyond teacher and pupil. These of themselves could not secure effective conditions of co-operation. After the teacher is enthroned in the school-room, he does much to secure and maintain conditions of unity; but up to that point, and continuous with his duty, society must secure and maintain the teacher in his place under conditions of successful labor. Schools are not detached from society, but are constantly conditioned by the educational thought and sentiment of the public. If the school goes wrong, it must ultimately be charged to public intelligence and purpose; but not immediately, for society realizes its thought and wish through executive agencies. What this thought and wish should be I have tried to deduce in the two preceding chapters. After these conditions have been clearly defined in thought and purpose, it yet remains to realize them; therefore the next step in the evolution of the school is to secure executive agencies to institute and maintain the school, giving rise to the problem of *school supervision*.

From the two factors in the school process, discussed in the two foregoing chapters, it is obvious that school supervision has two quite distinct phases,—one, that of supervising the conditions of instruction; the other, that of supervising instruction itself. The first is chiefly a business function, but it has also a professional aspect; for the conditions of instruction must be interpreted in order to supply them intelligently. The second requires strictly expert, professional skill. While these two functions have usually been performed by a single person called superintendent, city or county, it is hoped that, in due course of differentiation, there will arise soon distinct agencies for the distinct functions. But whether these two functions be exercised by one, or located in separate agents, they must be kept quite distinct in thought, both for clearness of discussion and efficiency of action.

Supervision of Instruction. — The aim of supervision of instruction is to secure the proper qualities in the teacher. The true teacher requires of himself the qualities the pupil demands; but, until he is a true teacher, he has not the knowledge and the spirit to make such requirement. Considering the weakness of human nature, it would not be safe to trust those interested to decide for themselves the question of fitness for admission into the profession. There must be some one competent and trustworthy to voice the unconscious demands of the child, and check, as would the child, the admission of the unworthy and incompetent. This becomes less necessary as the pupil approaches maturity; college and university students can largely be trusted to defend themselves. Under the elective system they starve out the indifferent teacher; yet protection here would be timely, in preventing the student's starvation along with that of his teacher. Neither can the public, who create and support the school by a strong educational sentiment, specify the needs of the student definitely enough to guide in securing the proper qualities in the teacher. The general theories of the public are too crude and indiscriminating to specify exactly what is needed. And if this were not true, function must be located to be executed.

This one, to stand for the pupil as over against the teacher, and to define and voice the intelligence of the public, must be selected out of the ranks of the teachers themselves; for there is required of him the highest degree of the same kind of qualifications as that already described for the teacher. He must secure the qualifications in the teacher required by the growing life of the pupil; and for this he needs the same sympathy for the pupil, and the same insight into his life, as required of the teacher. He has the function of the teacher raised to the second power. He teaches through the teacher; and from the fact that he can test and guide many teachers, his influence on the pupil is multiplied manyfold beyond that of direct instruction.

In the process of evolution the superintendent's function becomes entangled with business which does not belong to a teacher. But he is always properly classed as a teacher; and when evolution has done its perfect work, he will be restricted to the supervision of teachers. The fact that so large a number who are called superintendents devote themselves chiefly to the business and political interests of the school is incidental to the situation; and no indication that such is the normal and final condition of things. The business side of the school must receive atttention; and since the superintendent is not always fully differentiated in his preparation, he devotes himself to the business phase of school work, it being more tangible and less rigid in its requirements. At present the superintendent has combined in him both functions, giving most emphasis, perhaps, to business, — such as looking after supplies, or inspecting attendance and promotion records — the business-educational part of the program. Since there must be a business man, those who have more taste and skill for the external affairs of the school should be restricted to that department of work, leaving to those who have the more highly specialized professional skill the work of supervising instruction.

Such differentiation is rapidly going on, and in many schools, although not yet legally recognized, it has virtually taken place. Superintendents, overburdened with business affairs, or feeling unsafe in assuming to direct scientific instruction, are securing supervisors of primary work and of special subjects, and also the aid of an assistant superintendent who exercises general supervision over instruction. While law can do but little to hasten any form of social progress till that progress becomes largely an accomplished fact there is a stage in the process when legal recognition gives instant relief to the struggling forces. This relief has been felt in the school of Cleveland, Ohio, which recently took the final step, the superintendent receiving the legal title, Superintendent of Instruction, the business management being intrusted to a Director. These receive equal salaries, and have absolute power in their respective functions, the superintendent being appointed for life, or during good behavior.

It seems reckless to give a superintendent absolute power. Without a check, is there no danger of his becoming autocratic, and defiantly independent? The system, however, instead of being autocratic, is strictly democratic. Every child, parent, and educational interest stands in direct touch with the superintendent. He must shape his conduct from the standpoint of the child, as reflected, it may be, through the parent; he must justify his theory and his practice before the highest court of public appeal, — the people themselves. A superintendent who serves a board may, knowing its personal make-up, ingeniously fasten himself on the system in many ways other than by efficient service; but when he comes before the educational public, he must address himself to the business in hand.

The unlimited superintendent, with man's natural love of power, might become intoxicated if it were not for the sobering fact of fearful responsibility. It would seem that such a position would be eagerly sought; but indeed, he is a bold man who makes the venture. Responsibility is always commensurate with liberty and opportunity; and fear naturally arises with the thought of absolute authority, which has to be justified by him who enjoys the authority. If the child has a poor teacher, the child, parent, and public can say, "You did it." When the tenure of office is conditioned on good behavior, coupled with personal responsibility, the situation is such as to put the superintendent on good behavior, because he must always face his own deed. If his deed justifies his opportunity, life is too short for such service; if not, he makes his own cause for removal.

While the situation requires all the pluck and self assurance a superintendent can muster, he will still have a large balance of joy in the opportunity of realizing cherished ideals. When ideals disturb, there is no elation of life so great as that arising from opportunity to realize them; and the ecstasy which accompanies the labor is the sustaining power and sufficient reward of the laborer. A superintendent who does not feel deeply the burden of responsibility, does not comprehend the requirements of his vocation, and is not qualified for the duties before him. But if the hesitancy thus produced is not overcome by confidence founded in a firm conception of the educative process, and by the hope of realizing his educational ideals through the opportunity offered, still more should we suspect some fundamental defect in his professional character.

The first step in securing the proper teaching qualities is that of: —

Selecting the Teacher. — This, aside from the act of teaching, is the most critical function of the organism. The one held responsible for this duty must know, in a scientific and professional way, the necessary qualifications of a teacher; and besides, must have that devotion to the pupil which makes him firm against the importunities of the unqualified, whether they be relatives, friends, or home or foreign talent. There is but one law, and this requires that the best available teacher be secured, else the superintendent robs the tax-payer, and murders the child. Under the most favorable conditions, the supply of well-prepared teachers is always much too small; and to further limit by irrelevant bases of choice is an outrage on the pupil and the public. The greatest ethical strain of the system occurs at this point, and the appointing power must be located in a superintendent of rigid integrity and uncompromising educational convictions.

Of all the functions strictly belonging to the superintendent, that of selecting teachers is yet prominently shared by the board, just as the business of the board is shared by the superintendent. However, the long contention of the superintendent with the board for his professional rights has left with the board, generally, only the privilege of formal approval of the superintendent's actions. This satisfies the board, as they may still claim the power; while the superintendent is comfortably screened behind the board assuming his action. The superintendent may desire the evolution to go no further; but this would be to permit him to escape still the responsibility which the nature of the organism requires. He must exercise the appointing power undisguised, if he expects opportunity for the highest professional effort.

The first test of a superintendent, city or county, or of a president of a college or university, lies in the kind of teacher put in and kept in the school. Nowhere can he show better, or worse, judgment; and nowhere else more, or less, of earnest educational conviction and downright honesty of purpose. Of course the embarrassment is great; for always the supply of teachers, of the kind demanded, falls far short of the demand. Hence the earnest plea for professional schools. Such schools are doubly grounded: first, in the necessity for the individual to prepare himself for the profession; and second, in the necessity of the superintendent in securing trained teachers. These complementary forces are yet to work together more effectively in establishing more numerous and more efficient schools for elevating the professional status of the teacher. The purpose of such schools being to train teachers, the discussion under the "Unifying Qualities in the Teacher" suggests the general character and scope of their work. At this point we are interested only in their organic place in the system.

After the superintendent has made the best possible selection under the limitations, he will have to exercise still another function, that of: —

Aiding the Teacher. — While the function of helping the teacher belongs to the superintendent, this fact ought not to encourage the policy of employing cheap teachers and a high-priced superintendent, expecting him to reach the pupil through inferior instruments. Since the most efficient superintendent may exhaust his efforts through the most skilful teachers which can be secured, the foregoing policy necessarily lowers the standard of school work.

If direct and immediate help to inefficient teachers could be eliminated, the superintendent still has the problem of the continued growth of those teachers who were very desirable at the time of selection. An ideal teacher is not one who has reached perfection, but one at the upper limit of the profession pushing vigorously for better things. Such a one is most dissatisfied with present attainments, and presses most eagerly for assistance. At any rate, with all grades of teachers the superintendent's best service is not in direct suggestion, but in general guidance and stimulus to higher professional life. There must be constant unsettling through the revelation of higher ideals and more scientific processes. The teacher's work will improve only under rational insight into educative processes, and not by direct advice and authority of the superintendent. Teachers are too prone to seek what a superintendent desires, in order that they may conform to his wishes. This may arise from lack of definite conception of the work in hand, or from a desire to stand well with authority. And superintendents understand too well how to manipulate this weakness. The obedience which the superintendent should cultivate in the teacher is that of obedience to the reason in the educative process. The superintendent should completely obscure himself as authority, but become conspicuous as a leader of thought. As the pupil looks to the teacher for the higher life of culture, so should the teacher look to the superintendent for the higher life of the profession. The unity between the teacher and the superintendent should be as organic and sympathetic as that between the pupil and the teacher.

But it must not be inferred that a superintendent is superior to the teacher; his knowledge and skill are different in kind, but not necessarily in degree. A super-intendent may serve wisely teachers who excel him in the details of their work; in fact, they should be expected to so excel him. Surely, in the ideal condition of things, there will be as much general culture and professional knowledge and skill in the teacher of a grade, as in a superintendent; but the special preparation will be different. The preparation of a college president is different from that of a member of his faculty; but this does not require on his part a higher degree of culture or professional attainment. The unjust discrepancy between the pay of a superintendent and the grade teacher, and that between a president and member of his faculty, cannot be justified wholly by the difference in the qualifications required; the great advantage given to one must be partly accounted for by the mere accident of occupying a conspicuous and authoritative position. This accident, too, often persuades the mediocre superintendent to assume an unbecoming superiority. Under this delusion he moves about with an air of omniscience, making wise, commonplace remarks; and negative, cutting, personal criticisms. In the intervals he looks after the condition of blackboards and school-rooms, and inspects records and programs, and does whatever easy work he can pick up to keep himself busy. His professional criticisms suggest surcharged wisdom, but only wound and embarrass those he should help. All of this is a violation of the law of unity, which forbids the superintendent to stand over against the teacher, but which requires the closest sympathetic co-operation between them. As the teacher operates by fusion with the pupil's life, so the superintendent must become one with the teacher, and through the teacher with the pupil. The superintendent's function is to bring the teacher into unity with the pupil; and this, since the teacher must become one with the pupil, he cannot do except by unity with the teacher. To supervise instruction is to find the way through the teacher to the pupil. It must be as if the superintendent taught the pupil himself, having the practical skill of the teacher added to his broader conceptions of theory. Whatever higher conceptions he may have of the life-giving functions of the subjects to be taught must, through his agency, come into the life of the pupil. While the superintendent teaches at long range and through multiplied instrumentalities, he must touch the life of each individual pupil. It is too common to find a superintendent with good theories of the process of instruction in a given subject while none of the better things are seen bearing their fruit. A superintendent is not a superintendent unless his best conceptions of educative processes find their way through the teacher into the life of the pupil. This does not mean that the teacher is to become a mere instrument of transmission, but must yet remain a potent personal originating force. Here, as before suggested, the superintendent can do harm by pushing his theories onto the teacher more rapidly than they can be organized into an originating force of the teacher's own. While the teacher is the superintendent's leverage of reaching the mass of pupils, and of doing more effectively the direct work than he himself could do, this instrument must be taken in no mechanical sense; but as an original throbbing life, charged with its own message to the pupil.   Ultimately, what the superintendent is held for is the kind of work the pupil is receiving, — not his elaborate reports and published theories. The test is, whether his own best thought of teaching reaches the pupil through the teacher as if the teacher himself originated it.   He must make the teacher the active force and applier of his own best educational conceptions.

Thus the same law of unity between teacher and pupil holds for the superintendent. But with him it is much more difficult to fulfil ; for many more instrumentalities intervene between him and the pupil. Not only the teacher, but also the material conditions of the teacher's labor, and often the political machinery of the school, intercept his movement toward the pupil. One of the great problems of educational reform is that of conserving supervising energy   This consists first in removing the temptation for the superintendent to spend his days and nights in securing the election of members of the school board who will serve his personal ends, and after election to redouble his diligence to manage them instead of the school. The next step is that of relegating to business men and clerks the business and routine side of school work, so that the superintendent must justify himself by his own special work, rather than by a multitude of indefinite duties cleverly performed. And lastly, there must be selected a superintendent with a clearly defined educational character, rather than a man of heterogeneous and conflicting elements required in dealing with the concrete situations of business and politics, while managing the educational interests of the school. Thus might we hope to find more uniformly men of commanding eminence filling the school position, of all others most potent for good, because widest and most searching in its influence.

Supervising Conditions of Instruction. — While the business agent is supposed to be skilled in providing the necessary conditions, the teacher and superintendent must specify them; for one who does not know the educative process cannot specify the conditions of that process. Thus the business agency of the school, which selects and authorizes the teacher and superintendent, in turn becomes subject to the direction and authority of that teacher and superintendent. Through the organic relation of conditions to the teaching act, the teacher must keep before the board the conditions next most needed, that school funds may be most effectively distributed. Boards waste much in buying and contracting at random, and under the persuasion of interested agents. A board acts ill-advisedly in buying six tellurian globes, when a dictionary has not been supplied. The question is not what is a good thing for a school, but what is now most needed. Only the teacher and the superintendent can be expected to know this; and it is their duty, through a knowledge of the conditions as organized and working to the teaching act,

7

to keep before the proper authorities the most effective ways of expenditure.

But while the teacher knows what is needed, he cannot be expected to procure it. He should know the appointments of a school-house, and that it should be kept in a cleanly and orderly condition; but he cannot be expected to act as janitor or architect, or to enter into business relations with them. At this point arises the need of special business knowledge and skill, and calls for a new organ in the system.

The differentiation of this function and that of superintendent has already been discussed. The business side of the school process, as well as that of the supervision of instruction, is one of the professional aspects of school work, and should be dignified by a salaried official. What has been said touching the opportunity and responsibility of a differentiated superintendent, holds with as much force for a differentiated school director. If money is wasted or a contract fraudulently filled, the responsible source can be directly located. A man whose profession is to supply conditions of school work is apt to use all diligence in keeping his trust; but if he serve incidentally, as a citizen with other citizens, interest and responsibility are at lowest tension.

In this and the previous discussion of the differentiation of the supervising forces, and the separate location of functions in superintendent and director, I have not, of course, described the actual conditions of things, but only the ideal order of evolution, which is already indicated in advancing types of the system. Only by speaking to the ideal can the discussion be practical. The principle of guidance for the director of a country school, the township trustee, or the school board of a village or city must be found in their ideal relations to the teaching process, which requires the distinct embodiment in a specialized officer. Whether things are so or can now be made so, is not the question; but what is the ideal requirement of the law of the school, so that the duty may be clearly discerned, and as fully performed as entangling relations permit. If the genesis of the organism under the law moves inevitably to the differentiation of the supervising function into that of superintendent and director, we have the most significant fact for the immediate guidance of all school officers, and for giving future trend to the organism.[1]

Basis and Limitations of Supervision. — Public opinion is both the basis and limitation of supervision. The director, appointing the superintendent by the approval of a board who represent the people, is the immediate connecting link between the school and public sentiment. But when appointed, the superintendent shares the mediating function between the school in its concrete reality and public opinion. These special executive agents serve

---

[1] Since completing this discussion, the Report of the Committee of Fifteen has appeared, containing a sub-report on " The Organization of City School Systems." This sub-report is a more comprehensive statement and a stronger enforcement of the ideal here presented than I have been able to make.

under the legislative action, which emanates from society as a whole. While insisting that executive function must be centralized in a single officer, it is also recognized that a widespread and intelligent school sentiment, from which may come wise school legislation, is, after all, the real basis of the school. The more people who take an active interest in school the better. Diffusion of educational sentiment is as necessary as definite location of executive function. Wide diversity of intelligent conviction, focused in unity of action, is the only means to certain, permanent, and valuable results.

The executive officers, being limited by the conditions imposed by the public, cannot be held responsible beyond the limits of opportunity furnished. Aside from lack of general encouragement and recognition of worthy service, the limitations are of two specific kinds. Society may fail to supply a sufficient number of competent teachers, and thus force the superintendent to choose inferior ones; or fail to supply funds sufficient to secure the best talent when found, or to furnish the proper conditions for effective service. The superintendent is doubly limited over the business agent; for he cannot find so easily what he wants, or secure it when found. Besides, it is much easier, it seems, to secure funds to supply the material conditions of the school than to secure the best professional service. The former is more tangible and conspicuous. A teacher is supposed to be a teacher, and that is the end of the matter. The distinctions in finer qualities, which are vital to the pupil, are not patent to the public gaze, or discernible by the unskilled eye. The old wooden school-house can easily be replaced with a brick structure, with turret and bell; while the wooden teacher remains undisturbed. Public sentiment must be educated, if not into a clear discernment of professional qualifications, into a faith that there is all the difference in the world between a scientific teacher working under proper conditions and just anybody teaching under any conditions. Schools are not good just in proportion to the money expended on them,— not at all; but the wisest supervision cannot make a good school without ample provision of funds, nor unless society furnishes a sufficient number of well-trained teachers. Public sentiment must be so quickened that it will not tolerate poor schools, and at the same time be made to feel responsible for the conditions which may produce good ones. The school cannot progress out of touch with the life that supports it. Ultimately, what is good in the school must be accredited to society; and there, too, must rest the blame for its shortcomings.

And now we can retreat no further. If the student is not realizing himself daily, we look at once to the teacher, primarily; and then to the conditions under which he labors. Having located the evil in one or the other of these, we then turn to hold the proper supervising agency responsible. He must correct the evil, or show that the conditions imposed on him by the public make the remedy impossible. If the latter, nothing is left but to educate public sentiment and wait for the course of time to bring the remedy.   In this it appears the duty of every educational man to be diligent in moulding educational sentiment, and in giving trend to educational thought.   His professional duty is not circumscribed to the school-room or the office; he must face about and voice to the public their own latent ideas and purposes, and crystallize their convictions into active educational forces.

THE ORGANISM EXECUTING THE LAW.

WHILE the organism extends out to the limit of the school consciousness, and includes the whole of society, the focal centre of the organism is in the unity of teacher and pupil; and the work of the organism is executed in this active unity, for which we have been preparing. The teacher, with qualifications as before enumerated, now confronts pupils under the conditions as before specified; and the school which existed only in the thought and purpose of society becomes a concrete, living, moving reality.

The school is now in the active process of realizing the instruction for which it was organized; but in the process it secures an end not in the idea which gave birth to the organism. While the school, as does a machine, consumes much of the energy which it is supposed to apply, yet it makes good the loss in being an educative force in and of itself. In this case the instrument is not something apart from the material on which it operates. The pupil to be taught is a part of the instrument by which he is taught; the institutional life is his own life, and he is necessarily trained into certain forms, habits, and principles of ethical conduct. While the school is primarily organized to give instruction in all that pertains to human life and human welfare, including morals, it happens that the power of the school in ethical training, inherent in the organism itself, more than compensates for the friction of the organism; and this must be taken into the account when estimating educative forces.

The organism, then, in executing the law, does so by serving as a means of instruction; and, while doing so, it trains the pupil in rational self-control and in the spirit and forms of institutional life. While ethical teaching belongs to the regular course of instruction, and not to the subject of school management, the ethical training which comes from efficient school management must be given due prominence. Both results — instruction and ethical training — are secured in the same process; and the management which is best for one is most efficient for the other. While for clearness of discussion they must be treated separately, and, therefore, one before the other, the co-existence of the two processes must not be forgotten. Since instruction is the initiative force and the basis of the movement, it is proper to consider first the organism as executing the law through instruction.

The Organism in the Process of Instruction.

In this process the teacher moves in unity with the school as a whole, or in sub-unity with parts; as, with class studying or reciting.

Unity in School as a Whole. — Many things the school, as a whole, join in doing, — such as devotional exercises, gymnastics, passing in and out of school-room, etc. In all such the pupils should be required to act and think as one. In all general exercises too much care cannot be taken to have, at the outset, the attitude of attention; everything else must be put aside. The desks should be cleared of needless books and articles, and the whole room assume the appearance of unity. When an announcement is to be made, or a direction is to be given, the teacher should not utter a word of it till sure that every one is attentive. The combined movement of putting books in desks, in turning, standing, marching in and out of the room, is conducive to both order and discipline, as well as being a great economy of time.

But caution is here needed. Machinery should not be introduced for its own sake; it is always an inner unity that is desired, and formality is destructive of this. The outer form must be a necessity of the inner spirit. The teacher must rationally decide, having all the circumstances and conditions of the particular school at hand, just what mechanical combinations result from the inner necessity. The teacher cannot take this from imitation, or from any statement that might be made; for special conditions would give a new form to the law of unity. A country school with all grades must be managed differently from a room of two grades in a city school, or from a high school or college. All that is needed is the principle, and common-sense.

But while warning the teacher against machinery for its own sake, danger also lies in the other direction, — too little attention to the military side of the school. It is sometimes urged that putting away books, moving in and out, etc., by signals, interferes with the pupil's individuality. We ought to think twice before being alarmed at this. This so-called individuality is just what needs breaking into. The child will be a member of society after a while, and then will have to fall into line, and march to the music of the social order. Caprice and wilfulness cannot be interfered with too much; and the requirements of strict combination take square issue with these. The child lacks the power of self-control, and cannot bring himself into harmony with others. This of itself would be ground for the most rigid requirement of unity, to say nothing of facilitating school work and making instruction effective. But this anticipates the ethical value of school management.

It must not be supposed that when a teacher passes to class work, he leaves the school as a whole; in dealing with the class he must not drop out of sight the whole of which the class is a part. Securing unity in the school as a whole is a continuous process, and requires constant tension in the teacher. Hence the teacher needs to be well reinforced by that element of professional spirit called sensitiveness to unity in the organism. All the conditions enumerated may be perfect, but they will go for naught unless the teacher who stands before that school has the sense and habit of organic unity in thought.

He must constantly grasp the school into unity as the work proceeds; and this requires, as already discussed, a power of a definite kind, — the power to hold all the details of the process without losing sight of the main issue. The teacher must have a potent ideal of unity, — an ideal which really orders everything into an harmonious system. Unless this be true, the school goes loose all through, and the teacher, while he may feel vaguely that something is wrong, cannot discern definitely what it is. With this feeling of unity there must be the power to grasp the classes and the individuals as parts into the unity of the whole. The curtain must be adjusted, the room ventilated, the temperature regulated, the pupil answered, the recitation heard, and with these the whole school move forward in the mind of the teacher.

And now, in the presence of the pupils, the teacher must not only think and feel the school as a unit, but must draw the pupils into unity with himself by the power of sympathy. The teacher may grasp intellectually the school as one; and yet, in doing so, may hold pupils off at arm's length. Be it remembered that the unity desired is that between mind of teacher and pupil; and this can be secured only when the teacher's sympathy reaches out and draws the pupil to himself. The warmth of the teacher's life must be felt by the pupil; there must be no cold atmosphere between them. The teacher's heart must yearn for the pupil's highest good. If the teacher is really interested in the lives of his pupils, — all aglow with sympathy in their struggles, — they, by the law of sympathy, will be quickened into new life by the vital touch of mind with mind. This is the unity sought, and can never be realized by any except by the sincere and true-hearted teacher.

And thus, as the teacher moves forward from moment to moment, and from hour to hour, with the complex organism, and with multifarious duties, he must have at all times an abiding consciousness of the unity of the whole, and be in constant, rigid exercise of unifying power.

The pupils before the teacher, and who are now to join with him, have, through difference in age and training, quite diverse abilities. All these must join with the teacher in the act of instruction; yet the difference in ability may be so great that all cannot join in the same act, thus requiring the teacher to perform different acts in adaptation to different classes of pupils. This introduces the most distressing problem, especially in the country schools, with which the teacher and superintendent have to deal, — namely, that of classification and gradation, which, together, constitute, in the restricted sense, school organization. Hence there must be, preparatory to the actual teaching, and continuous with it, the: —

Organization of the School.

Organization has, primarily, reference to the relation of pupils to teacher, and not to the relation of pupils to each other; the resulting secondary arrangements among pupils is of little or no consequence. This, like grasping the school as a whole while conducting the recitation, is a process continuous with instruction. A school organ-organized does not remain so, but from day to day needs constant re-adjustment. The yearly paroxysms of examinations and promotions do not indicate the continuous and healthful re-adjustment required by the law of unity.

A school is organized when pupils are classed and graded, and when the movement of the whole is programmed.

Classification. — All pupils who join with the teacher in the same act at the same time form a class; when this class is thought of as joining with the teacher in a series of acts in the development of a subject, it is called a grade. Thus a grade and a class are one and the same thing, differing only in the view taken; in the class the learning acts are viewed as simultaneous, while in the grade, learning acts are viewed as successive. The same group of pupils, viewed in the two relations, forms both the class and the grade.

A class is the result of an organization, and not itself an organization. Organization is the co-operative relation between teacher and pupil. Several pupils may co-operate — be organized — with the teacher at the same time. These, having the same attributes of co-operating, form a class, — just as birds having the same attribute, blue, form a class, blue birds. Class unity is thus incidental, and of no direct educational service further than that of indicating the organic unity between teacher and pupil. The latter is primary and must be secured, at whatever cost to external uniformity in classification. The ignoring of this distinction, and forcing external class unity, is the source of all the evils of the class system. Organic unity may prevent the uniform constituency of a class as the teacher changes from one subject to another. A pupil is a member of a class by virtue of his unity with the teacher; his connection with the particular members of the class is a matter of indifference. The first is vital; the second formal.

Therefore such pupils as can join with the teacher in a given line of thought should constitute a class. These are determined not only by the qualifications of the pupils, but by the number the teacher can grasp in the process of instruction. The teacher has come to instruct more than one at a time under the force of economy, and not under the command of an educational principle. Whatever gain there may be in class association, this is not taken as a determining principle of instructing many at once. Certainly the overcrowded condition of classes can only be explained on financial grounds, as illustrated by the difference between the size of classes in an endowed university and in a private school supported by the tuition of students.

The difficulty of instructing by classes, both because of number and inequality of pupils, and by further reason of the abuse of the class system, has caused a reaction in favor of the old plan of individual instruction, — as, for instance, in Pueblo, Col., where the pendulum has made its complete rebound.   Individual instruction is the newest current topic touching the question of classification.   The assumption is that classification necessarily opposes efficient instruction.   Since no two pupils are exactly alike in knowledge and power, when the teacher adjusts his mind to one it is not exactly adjusted to the other.   Hence perfect organization seems to destroy the class altogether; but this is only a seeming.

The practicability of individual instruction is questionable, and closer analysis makes it appear undesirable. The reaction against class instruction comes largely from the abuse of the system, and not from objections inherent in the system itself.   When classification and gradation were new features of the school system, naturally they were exalted into ends to which the pupil was means. Mechanical system compressed the free life of the pupil, and classification was censured for the sins of uniformity. The abuse of the system must not condemn it, and its inherent difficulties may be offset by its inherent advantages.

The assumption that class instruction is not individual instruction insinuates itself through the opposition of terms, — class and individual.   All instruction must be individual instruction.   To teach a class is to teach the individuals composing it, and not some substituted abstraction.   It is possible to form a class so that the needs of each member may be as fully met as if each had his own teacher. Quite a wide range of ability, especially in upper classes, is consistent with individual instruction in classes. Absolute uniformity is necessary only for those teachers who force pupils to square-inch text-book results; but the teacher who puts flexible and living problems to the class may engage strong pupils to their utmost capacity, while the weakest work to advantage. In a town school of five hundred pupils, a class, as large as any class should be, can be formed of pupils so nearly equal in ability that the teacher who properly assigns work will experience no inconvenience in teaching them; but rather will feel reinforced by the enlarged complex life and spirit of the class.

The Pueblo plan, as described in the "Educational Review," February, 1894, while challenging discussion in its details, and in the principle assumed, sounds the true keynote of organization in the following paragraph: —

"The fundamental characteristic of the plan on which the schools are organized is its conservation of the individual. The pupil is placed purely with reference to where he can get the most good for himself; he works as an individual, progresses as an individual, is promoted as an individual, and is graduated as an individual. The ordinary nomenclature of schools is continued for convenience; but the school system is one of flexibility, permitting pupils to pass from working-section to working-section as may be expedient. The perplexities relative to class intervals have disappeared, because there is no mechanical classification. In appellation the term junior or senior may be used; but such term does not locate the individual any more than the name of a division of a railroad locates the exact position of a particular train. For working purposes the pupils are grouped in working-sections; but the members of a working-section are not necessarily doing the same work, or rather they are not doing the same work simultaneously. In brief, the school is both graded and ungraded, — graded in so far as applies to its plan of work, but ungraded in its accommodation of the individual."

This is new and refreshing in contrast with the stifling system of mechanical uniformity. Yet let it be noted that this cannot be a rude jostling and misplacing of the old. The new is generally, if not always, a return to that which is older than the old with which it is in conflict. Since there is nothing new under the sun, the new is really the old. The "Pueblo plan" is both new and old: it is new in being a protest and a reaction against the abuses of the graded system; it is old in that the plan is one of individual instruction. Some thirty years ago the "'Possum Kingdom School" was taught on the Pueblo plan, — pupils without classification receiving individual aid. I speak of no fictitious school, but one named, in those days innocent of methods and terminologies, not after its characteristic mode of instruction, but after the characteristic animal of the dense forest in which the school was located. If the teacher of that school should chance upon the Pueblo plan, he would exclaim: "What have you teachers been about all these years? Have n't you known all the time that you must teach the pupil, — the individual pupil? Sorry, indeed, that I did not write up the 'Possum Kingdom plan thirty years ago, and hasten the arrival of the great doctrine of individual instruction.

From the individual plan, through gradation and classification, back to the individual plan, — from 'Possum Kingdom to Pueblo, — what does it mean? Certainly it means a check on the abuses of the graded system; and it ought to mean much more; namely, that class instruction, with all of its merits, is harmonized with the needs of each individual in the class. It should mean class instruction and individual instruction at the same time. The Pueblo plan must not be too literally a return to the 'Possum Kingdom plan; but must bring a contribution from years of experience with the graded system. Pupils may be taught in classes without interfering with the rights of the individual; and thus, indeed, really further the interests of the individual more than can be done by individual instruction. So that, while we protest against the abuses of arbitrary gradation and classification, we must be careful to add what is good in it to the old plan of individual instruction. The new must return to the old with increase, for "through the ages one increasing purpose runs," and the old must be "widened with the process of the suns."

Gradation. — While classification requires unity of each individual in the class with the teacher at a given moment in the act of teaching, gradation requires unity of each individual with the teacher in successive moments through the course of instruction. The first is a simultaneous unity; the second a successive one. The same pupil that joins with the teacher at a given moment may be unable to do so in successive moments; because pupils relatively vary in ability in different subjects, and from time to time in the same subject. Gradation thus conflicts with permanence and uniformity of classification; but not, however, with true classification; for true classification requires constant re-adjustment of class membership as much as does gradation. As a school is truly classified when the members of a class can join with the greatest profit in the same act of instruction, so a school is truly graded when each pupil in his forward movement follows the continuity of ideas determined by the natural growth of his mind. A graded school is not a school consisting of two or more rooms in the same building; but a school moving over a system of ideas graded by the pupil's law of development. Each class must be graded (*gradus*, a step); must move by an organic series of steps.

The possibility of grading country schools used to be questioned, forgetting that it was impossible to do anything else. This was not questioned in the town schools, because the different rooms of the school building made it necessary to block out the school in parts, called grades. This is the most superficial and mechanical sense of gradation. Closely allied to it is the notion of grades as being the time distances between classes. Not the school-room now, but the almanac, make the gradation. Grades were supposed at first to be classes a year apart in progress of studies; and later this distance was shortened to a half or a third of a year, the essential idea all the time being that regularity of distance in the course is essential to the graded system. From this resulted the evil practice of forcing and checking the natural speed of the class; feeling that all system is destroyed without adherence to mathematical measurements of space and time. Thus the calendar and the pages of the text usurp the rightful authority of the law of development. Since the pupil's growth is not endogenous, and by joints, gradation by the periodical joint system must be a violation of the pupil's law of growth. Whatever limitations may arise from practical necessity, these must not give law to gradation, but themselves must be adjusted to that law. The distance between classes is but an accidental result; and, taken as a law of guidance, can but work mischief. The only safe working conception is that of a single class, or pupil for that matter, thought of in continuous process of growth through the course of instruction.

The first step in gradation is to arrange the elements of subjects into naturally developing series in the experience of the pupil. Certain ideas of the earth, and of all other subjects, are adapted to the child in the first period of his course; and, because of the acquired ideas and increased abilities of the first period, other ideas are adapted to him in the second period; and so on to the close of school life. Such an arrangement of ideas in all the subjects — an arrangement from a small centre at the beginning of the school course, out to the circumference at the close of the course — constitutes a graded course of study. The development of such a course belongs to the subject of instruction rather than to management; and has been discussed in "The Philosophy of Teaching," under the topic, "The Process as a Complex Whole." The course of study is nothing but the process of teaching taken in its entire complexity, — the length, breadth, and depth of the educative process. Gradation of pupils assumes that such a course has been developed, and requires of school management only the adjustment of pupils to that course.

Since the course of study has both length and breadth, — both warp and woof, — pupils have to be adjusted to both, making the problem of gradation doubly difficult. The pupils who may move forward together in one line may not always be the same pupils who can best move together in another line. Thus the lateral movement in the course may re-adjust the longitudinal movement. And here, for the sake of class uniformity, violence is most frequently done to the individual. Not gradation, but uniformity, requires pupils who recite together in one subject to recite together in all; or, the classes in one part of a city or county to do at the same time just what those in another part are doing. No educational reason can be given for the external uniformity of two schools; or, of the corresponding successive classes of different years in the same school. The class, because the individuals are to combine in the teaching act, must be uniform in time and in the general preparation of the lesson; but that another teacher should be, at the same time, moving a class over the same part of the same subject, is not required by the law of organization; and may be prohibited by that law. Even uniformity of text is not, except to a very limited extent, required or desirable. The teacher who is free from the text, being possessed by the subject, will find diversity of texts quite desirable; except when examples for drill are needed, as frequently happens in arithmetic, grammar, and reading.

The inherent difficulties of classification and gradation are great enough without imposing mechanism and uniformity on the system. The teacher will have enough to do to see that all the pupils in a given class, in a given subject, without reference to any other subject or any other class, are so nearly of equal ability as to join profitably with the teacher in the same discussion. The problem is thus reduced to the question of the number of classes, and of having strong and weak pupils in the same class. In many cases it is only a choice between two evils. It may be impossible to secure the condition required; but the ideal to be striven for is that stated, as against mere external uniformity, which is always in conflict with true organization.

The inherent difficulty is much less in city schools; but these do not always make the most of their opportunity for close classification. It often happens, for instance, that all fifth-year pupils are held to the same work, even when there are so many of them that two or more classes have to be formed. If there are seventy-five pupils in a fifth-year grade, so that three classes must be formed, it is far better to gradually collect the strong pupils in one class, the weak in another, and those of medium ability in a middle class. And then each of these classes should be required to move up the inclined plane only so rapidly as the strength of pupils permits. There should be no straining after mile-posts. No matter whether a class reach a prescribed station; let the point reached by the close of the term or year be noted by the teacher, and the march be resumed from that point at the opening of the next session. This somewhat interferes with the externally beautiful system, but it favors the internal unity sought. Besides, a pupil may recite in different classes within the limits of an ideal organization. Unity and proper classification may require a pupil to recite reading in a fifth-reader class, and arithmetic with fourth-reader pupils ; even should such interfere with the external system.

While a course of study may be graded apart from any given school, the external gradation — the adjustment of pupils to the course — cannot be made till the particular school is given, and all the conditions are known. When the number of pupils is small, and distributed over all the common-school grades of work, the distribution of pupils differs from the arrangement required by a school having double the number of pupils on the same course of work, and taught by two teachers. And still more will the variation be when passing to a village school of three hundred pupils, taught by eight teachers. Thus the arrangement of pupils with reference to the course of study must be figured out when all the determining facts about the school to be graded are known. To show the method of doing this, I may be permitted to insert an illustration from "A Graded Course of Study," published in 1883, which was prepared for a school in a small city. The determining facts were these: The course of study comprehended twelve years, — from primary to high school inclusive. The attendance was about six hundred and fifty pupils; and these were taught by fourteen teachers. After spreading out the course of study as a basis, and having the foregoing facts in mind, the following sketch is given: —

"Now, imagine the pupils in this school, in an unbroken procession from the bottom to the top of this inclined plane, toiling upward, each doing the work best suited to his ability, and you will have a picture of a perfectly graded school. But, for purposes of efficient instruction, this unbroken procession is broken into groups, or sections, of about twenty or twenty-five in a group. Of the six hundred and fifty pupils in this school, there are twenty-six such groups; each but a short distance and a short time behind the other. At the bottom of the inclined plane the groups are nearer

together than at the top; because the number in the
procession decreases upward, and the groups would be
too small for practical purposes; and because, also,
pupils of a wider range of ability in the upper grades
than in the lower can be taught in a class. A few weeks'
difference between the progress of a pupil and of a class
in the lower grades is sufficient to prevent the pupil from
working with the class, while this would not be true in
the upper grades.

"For convenience these groups are collected into still
larger groups. Since it takes the average pupil about
twelve years to finish the course, the course is divided
into twelve equal parts; and the twenty-six small groups
are made into twelve larger ones. This gives the twelve
grades as usually spoken of. Each of the first six of
these years, or grades, is composed of three of the smaller
classes above described; the seventh and eighth of these
grades are each composed of two classes; and the last four
of one class each.

"On the basis of the kind of knowledge gained and
faculties exercised, these twelve grades are made into
three larger groups, called departments; each consisting
of four grades.

"For all of these divisions we have this diagram of the
school. Read from bottom upward: —

School. {

3. High School Department. {
4. Twelfth year or grade.
3. Eleventh year or grade.
2. Tenth year or grade.
1. Ninth year or grade.

2. Intermediate Department. {
4. Eighth year or grade. {
Section 2.
Section 1.

3. Seventh year or grade. {
Section 2.
Section 1.

2. Sixth year or grade. {
Section 3.
Section 2.
Section 1.

1. Fifth year or grade. {
Section 3.
Section 2.
Section 1.

1. Primary Department. {
4. Fourth year or grade. {
Section 3.
Section 2.
Section 1.

3. Third year or grade. {
Section 3.
Section 2.
Section 1.

2. Second year or grade. {
Section 3.
Section 2.
Section 1.

1. First year or grade. {
Section 3.
Section 2.
Section 1.

"The sections, or classes, doing a year's work are not necessarily doing the same term's work, as before indicated; but may be one term apart. This is to give flexibility to the system. Usually, all the pupils of any year are required to do the same work; but this forces very unequal pupils into the same classes, and makes promotions and demotions less practicable; since, if a pupil is demoted, he must fall back a year, or if promoted, he will have to skip a year. Besides, this plan is entirely unnecessary, except when a grade is only large enough to make one class. Then, we are to think of each section of each grade working independently of the others, and doing the work best suited to it. This gives threefold greater opportunity for classing each pupil correctly, than if all the classes of one grade were required to do the same work.

"Each class should be required to stay on a year's work till it is done. It often happens that a slow class will need a year and a term, or a year and a half, in which to do a year's work. Such a class ought to remain on a year's work till the work is done, but need not remain in the same room. A strong class may finish the work in less time than assigned, and should not be held back for slower classes. A pupil should be transferred from one class to another at any time when it is best for the pupil.

"In describing each class, the term and the year should be given, thus: third term, 4's; first term, 5's; meaning, respectively, the highest class in the fourth year, and the lowest class in the fifth year. Thus should a class be entered on the class-record; and this, with the statement of the work of that class in this course of study, will enable any one to know just where a class belongs, and what work it has done. When a parent receives a card stating that his child has passed on a certain term's work, and is promoted to the next, by reference to this course he may have a definite idea of his child's progress. This will enable him to measure that progress, not by the rooms, nor even by the grades passed through, but by the field of knowledge covered."

The foregoing is not given as a plan for any one to follow, but to emphasize the principle that the organization of the school must be kept mobile to its inner life. To one who is accustomed to wind up the machine, and to trust it to run itself for fixed periods, this constantly shifting condition of things will seem unsafe and troublesome. And troublesome it is, for no fixed plan can be followed; no two schools are alike; and the same school is continually shifting, requiring constant vigilance and nimble judgment on the part of the superintendent. New problems are ever arising, whose solution cannot be anticipated. For instance, by the foregoing scheme of organization it appears that, in passing from the sixth to the seventh grade, three classes must be combined into two; and in passing from the eighth grade to the high school, two classes must be combined into one. Now these combinations may have to be made at other points in the movement, sooner or later. But whenever they have to be made it will ever be a recurring question as to the best way of doing it. It might happen that the most advanced of the two classes to be combined into the first year's work of the high school could best spend the time in a general review, while waiting for the lower class — not necessarily the weaker one — to complete the requirements for high school admission. Or, this most advanced class might, say at the beginning of the eighth year's work, check their speed by pushing out further into details of their subject than is regularly required; thus checking movement to reach the high school at the same time as the lower class. Or, it might be advisable for the class, or some members of it, to have a vacation for whatever time is required for the other class to reach the high school; giving to such members of the class as desired directions for lines of private reading and investigation, or special studies in school. It might happen to be best for the lower class — which may be the stronger of the two — to push work more rapidly, and join the other class, even if some points in the work had to be skipped. Or, something of all of these might have to be done. There is no end to the possible solutions of the problems which may arise under a flexible system; and the superintendent must be constantly in the movement; he cannot retire, having fixed the system to run itself for a stated period. Of course it is much easier to manage an organization fixed in straight and hard grooves. It is a simple matter to require uniformly all classes, or groups of classes, to keep one year apart, and to promote yearly by examinations. And it all looks well, too,— so regular, so uniform, so systematic ; no tinkering with a machine which is constantly getting out of order. But life is not mechanism; the school is not a machine; and the superintendent is not a stem-winding attachment.

It is obvious how the simple fact of the size of the school modifies the foregoing scheme. If the school should be considerably larger than the foregoing, consisting of two or three ward schools the size of the above, the three sections might continue through the high school. If this larger school should be in one building, with the three sections in the high school, then there would be more than three sections in the lower grades; and the problem of combinations would arise again; having disappeared with two or three wards, having one high school.

It is evident also that had the number of pupils in this school been twice as large, and yet taught in the same building, there would have been twice as many divisions in each year's work, making it possible to have classes only one-half a term apart. But this would yield no great gain in flexibility of grading, because it will be found that when classes are only one term apart, the members of a class are of such even ability that the teacher will find no difficulty in satisfying individual needs. If the school had been twice as large, and divided into two wards, no change would be made in the arrangement of classes. It thus seems that a ward school consisting of about five hundred pupils below the high school, and taught by ten or eleven teachers, comes close to the ideal. A system of city schools is only a multiplication of such school units, organized into the centre of the system, — the high school.

If there had been only two-thirds as many pupils in this school, and taught by eight teachers, classes would have been one-half a year apart, — which would have been good, but not so good. Especially not so good if the two classes had been forced, as is generally done, to do the same work, simply because they belong to the same year. Passing below this attendance and teaching force, the difficulty of classification increases rapidly; and becomes greatest when a single teacher has charge of all grades covering the public school course to the high school; which often happens; and sometimes advanced classes are added for good count. This is the most abnormal and stubborn condition with which the teacher has to contend in organizing and instructing a so-called ungraded school. The foregoing standard applied will accomplish all that can be accomplished; and the teacher must not reproach himself for not being able to do the impossible. But the foregoing standard is just as necessary for a teacher in such unfavorable conditions as if serving under ideal ones. The whole problem is to secure the best compromise between number of classes and diverse ability in each class.

As to the number of classes for a teacher, two seems to be the ideal; for each class moves by alternations of study and recitation; and while the teacher is waiting for a class to prepare work, he may be hearing another class recite. No problem of organization is more easily solved, theoretically, than the proper number of classes for a teacher; but none more difficult of practical solution.

And the two classes should not be doing the same work; not only to secure better classification, as already indicated, but for reasons found in the process of instruction. The repetition of a lesson before a class who have heard it dulls the zest of both teacher and pupils, besides interfering with the best preparation on the part of pupils. But any number above two classes is an interference and a burden; in the case of young pupils, because the teacher cannot return to them as frequently as they need attention. The preparation time is longer than they can profitably use. It is a very great evil for a primary pupil just entering school to receive attention for only four short periods per day, the teacher each time having been engaged one hour with three or four other classes. And with mature pupils the evil is also great, because it is impossible to consider the subject in the time allotted. In one case the time for study is too great; in the other the time for recitation is too short. Thus, in many ways, the number and diversity of classes is the perplexing and unsurmountable difficulty in sparsely settled rural districts. In a city the fault is not in the number of classes, nor lack of opportunity to classify properly, but in the size of classes. The ideal is to have two classes of proper size, and a short distance apart in subject-matter. While insisting that they should be apart, the distance must not be great. A teacher could not easily adjust himself alternately to a primary and a high-school grade.

After the pupils are classified and graded, they must be continually re-adjusted as instruction proceeds. This is accomplished by promotions and demotions, either by classes or by pupils. A class progressively and imperceptibly promotes itself, and the formal act is nothing more than change of name; but the single pupil is put back or forward with another class. The old question of when to promote or demote a pupil is solved by the foregoing discussion. Undoubtedly a pupil should be changed from one class to another just as soon as his interest will thereby be subserved. There is no educational reason for consulting the almanac in this matter. Not the moon's phases, but the most effective unity is the criterion; and let the step be taken as soon as the need is discerned.

The necessity for promoting or demoting a pupil becomes apparent to the teacher in the regular daily work, without any test by special examination. That the formal, fearful, periodical examination to determine fitness for promotion should be abolished, and that in its stead should be substituted the test of daily work, is a foregone conclusion. Frequent written recitations, along with oral work, should constitute a continuous examination. Nothing is a better test than a regular recitation; unless value is attached to a long-impending crisis to secure desperate application, and heroic effort in the last onset.

The school is not completely organized and ready for movement without a systematic program of exercises. This cannot be made out till the preceding steps have been taken; and it cannot be delayed longer, for it is the last step which conditions active school work.

The Program. — The severest strain put upon the teacher is that of keeping himself in constant unity with all the classes composing the school. To this end there must be a systematic time schedule for the movement of the whole; without which there will be delays, collisions, and wrecks. The teacher must know in advance just what movements and connections are to be made during each session.

This, more than anything else, brings that confidence and equipoise in meeting new situations and changes of movement which enthrones the teacher as master of the situation. Each class and each pupil must be so well provided for beforehand that all may be kept constantly employed; and without any confusion or seeming effort on the part of the teacher. It is dangerous to trust to the spur of the moment; for the moment may come without a spur. To provide fully for new situations, many things must be anticipated which do not have to be met. Too many provisions can do no harm; too few may be fatal.

Especially is all this true on the first day of school, when a special program is required. This day is not more trying simply because the exercises are irregular, but because the teacher is new, and on trial before the public sentiment of the school. The teacher who can hold the fort on this day has achieved a victory which promises success throughout. This victory comes by the teacher quietly keeping the whole school moving in unity, while organizing parts for permanent work; and this can be secured only by fixing precisely in mind the successive and simultaneous steps of all the parts during the session of organization. It is not sufficient merely to write out the program; the first day's work must have been lived through in idea so frequently that the teacher moves through the work with the custom and ease of life. It is said that a criminal who is to be executed walks up the scaffold so constantly in idea while in his cell that, when he comes to walk in reality before the awe-stricken spectators, his tread is firm and steady. Thus men prepare for trying situations, and the first day of school is one of them. If the teacher has not lived the first day in idea more than what is required to write out its program, expecting to turn to the desk to see what is next to be done, he cannot move with unruffled confidence and steady power. Hence the first day of school, in all the details which bring the whole into constant unity, must become a part of the life of the teacher by antici-pation, prolonged thought, and meditation. For instance, the teacher must have decided, and must have gone through the performance in idea many times, just when and how he is to secure the names of the pupils; whether to pass around, as of old, and write down each name as the pupil gives it when called upon. Or, would such a process, engaging but one pupil at a time, permit dissolution of the school; and be fatal to that business dispatch which begets confidence in pupils and sense of power in the teacher. If the teacher expects to develop a lesson, and assign work to a class, he must be very sure that he has some good employment for every member of every other class. Such precautions neglected, embarrassment is sure to follow; and the teacher becomes a Zekle in "The Courtin'," who

> ". . . stood a spell on one foot fust,
> Then stood a spell on t' other,
> An' on which one he felt the wust,
> He could n't ha' told ye nuther."

With such lack of poise and precision of movement, the pupils will feel by the close of the first day that the school is in weak hands; and so would the critical observer, for this is the real keynote of the teacher's managing ability.

But, after the school is well started, the systematic movement by regular program is essential to order and dispatch of work; unity of the whole being the constant and absolute requirement. The problem is to keep every pupil of every class at work all the time, wasting no time and energy, whatever the teacher may need to turn to. This is more than the problem of class unity; it is that of the unity of all the classes in the school movement as a whole. To this end the teacher must move systematically by a daily program; not necessarily by the same, perhaps necessarily not; but the exact written program must be the basis, from which variation may be made when occasion requires. Hence, however varying the life and movement of the school may be, the teacher must fix a scheme of class movements.

In this he must be especially careful to provide for the

study period, the class reciting being sure of engagement. Until recently the teacher gave little attention to this point; thinking that teaching is hearing the recitation, he left pupils to shift for themselves while out of it. But now we understand that the teacher shows at least as much skill, and serves the pupil as efficiently, in providing employment as in hearing the lesson. So that what the pupils are to accomplish during study time must be as definitely put into the program as the topic of recitation. The written program, however, can show the employment only in general; the program for each day, as well as for the first day, must be made out daily. Nothing can so much insure success for any day's work, as time spent on the evening or morning before each day, in setting up for guidance and inspiration the ideal performance for the day. Thus only can be insured precision of action, and certainty and force in execution.

Pupils in Active Unity with Teacher.

Whether or not there be one or more classes in charge of a single teacher, the work moves by alternate periods of study and recitation; and the teacher must strive as carefully to secure unity with pupils in the preparation of work as with those reciting.

Unity in Class Studying. — The ideal to be secured in the class, or classes, studying is the undivided and the greatest possible stress of attention during the study period on the thought assigned to be worked out. This is unity, not primarily of pupils among themselves, but with the teacher; although the teacher may at the time be studying, or conducting a recitation.

1. The first matter to receive attention is the condition of pupils before they are set to work. These conditions have already been enumerated, and are supposed to be supplied in general; but they must be continually re-adjusted at every breathing space in the work; especially at the beginning of the study and the recitation periods. All immediate physical wants of the pupils must be relieved, by attention to the condition of the room, and by recreation through rest and gymnastic exercise. A song before beginning study is a most potent means of reviving the spirits and toning the mind for the study hour. The teacher cannot afford to neglect any means which brings comfort and vigor and unity of mood to pupils before turning them to the preparation of the next lesson. The brief, spirited exercise and song more than compensate for the time consumed. The teacher who aspires to skillful management must not tire of little things, but must be alert to every detail of conditions which focuses energy on the work in hand.

2. The condition and attitude of pupils now favoring work, the assignment of the lesson is in order. Since teacher and pupils are to be one in the preparation of the lesson, the teacher, before it is possible to assign the lesson effectively, must have traced out all the thought relations in the subject assigned, which he wishes the pupil to trace out. If the teacher assigns the lesson by

pages, without being conscious of the thought effort required in mastering what is assigned, there can be no unity. Without such preparation on the part of the teacher, it would be a mere accident if the lesson were assigned so as to secure efficient effort on the part of the pupil.

Let it be noted again that the unity desired is, primarily, not that among pupils, but that between pupils and teacher. If the pupils focus their attention on the thought which the teacher has planned for them, unity among themselves will be incidentally secured. The unity essential may be secured by pupils studying at different times and places, as is done with college students. The only reason for requiring the pupils of common-school grades to study by program, at a given time and place, is that they have not the power to impose their own limit of time and place. This is the principle involved in the discussion of whether high school students should study at home. This question does not arise with the primary grade, nor with the seniors in a college; because the first without question cannot limit themselves to their task, while the second can do so. The primary pupil is to be trained into the power of self-limitation by imposing limits upon him. Since we scarcely know what to do with high school pupils in this respect, they must be in the transitional phase. The decision turns on whether they are so disciplined that they can self-impose their own task.

But the unity to be secured in the class studying,

whether by strict requirement of time and place, by program in the school-room, or by independent self-direction as to time and place, is the unity with the teacher in the thought to be worked out in the lesson. This brings our attention to one of the essential conditions of unity in the class studying, which is, that the lesson must first have been fully experienced by the teacher before assigning it for study by the class.

Teachers have learned fairly well that the preparation of a lesson is necessary in the recitation; but there is yet great need of conviction that careful preparation of a lesson is also essential to its proper assignment. This error arises, as do most others, from a false conception of the process of teaching. When teaching is conceived as a mechanical process of imparting results measurable by some special standard, as length of paragraph or page, then the lesson can be assigned by length and breadth of printed matter, and without any previous preparation other than eye measurement. But to measure the thought to be compassed by the pupil, requires a detailed preparation of the lesson as a condition of intelligent assignment.

3. The lesson should be so clearly and definitely assigned that the pupil can neither mistake nor escape what is to be done. It is well to have several pupils state just what is to be worked out during the study time; or, a better form, to require each of several to state just what he expects to work out during the time. Often a written assignment of the lesson on the board will hold the pupils

to more definite study, and the teacher to more definite assignment. This is a vital point in securing order; and the teacher must not feel that time is wasted in causing the pupils to put clearly and fully before themselves a specific topic, and a problem concerning it, which they are to work out.

This guards the pupil against supposing that the preparation of his lesson consists in mastering the form of what is said; or that it is limited to the outline of thought as the text must necessarily put it. He will thus be influenced to the use of reference books and library, and have his views enlarged and liberalized concerning the topic under discussion. The study period, as well as the recitation, is the teacher's opportunity to train pupils to proper habits of thought and investigation; and the teacher must recognize and improve the opportunity as much in the one case as in the other.

4. After each pupil has decided just what he is going to do, he must note whether he has all things needed for the work, and whether anything about him is not needed. All unnecessary things must be removed, and the pupil supplied with all that he may chance to need in the preparation of his lesson. If he is cold or thirsty, now is the time to attend to his wants. He must know that after the class has begun the lesson, he cannot get a pencil, fix the fire, or borrow a knife; that he must speak before the signal for work, or ever after hold his peace.

5. When each mind is made clear as to the work to be done, and all the wants have been supplied, some quiet

signal, as a nod, — all the pupils attentive to the teacher, — should be given for work to begin. The teacher should now pause before the class till he feels that all are in firm tension with the lesson. It is waste of time to be in nervous haste to pass to the recitation. A moment's pause and a quiet withdrawal strongly favor continued attention during the absence of the teacher.

6. While the teacher is conducting a recitation, no pupil in the class not reciting should be permitted to change work, speak to any one, get anything which should have been before supplied, fix the fire, ask the teacher about his lesson, etc. If the teacher has carefully provided for all the pupil's wants there can be no necessity for giving him attention now. To stop the recitation to answer his question is to give the time of the twenty in the class to the one. He has no right to break the unity between the teacher and the class. If he finds now that he needs a pencil, to supply him would cultivate a want of foresight; and by to-morrow he will want both pencil and book. He cannot get the pencil during the study time without breaking up the whole school, for a moment, at least. If he should pass to get a drink, or fix the fire, all work must stop for his convenience. His study time will, perhaps, continue not over thirty minutes; and if the teacher has attended to all wants, as he should have done, the pupil will not die for anything in so short a time, however warmly he may plead his cause. I do not mean that there are no circumstances under which the pupil may move and accommodate himself to his work. If the stove becomes too warm, or

if he needs to consult reference books, he should move from his desk without asking the teacher. It is a great gain in discipline and self-control for the pupil to take himself in charge so far as possible. We must not have foolish notions about obedience, and give the pupil to understand that he must not breathe without permission from head-quarters. Freedom of the pupil under his own judgment as to what is proper is the only way to secure the unity desired, and to cultivate the power of self-control.

It is not quite so clear that the pupil should not change his work during the study time of a given lesson. Suppose a strong pupil gets his history lesson in half the time assigned, should he not turn to some other lesson? This is better than for him to sit idle, or be stirring up fun. The fallacy is in the supposition. He has not his lesson, if it be well assigned. If so many paragraphs are given to learn, he may commit them, and, having a watch with stop attachment, may note the second and fraction of a second in which he made the course. But I have in mind a real teacher, who gives the class a problem to work out; and a problem is elastic. Suppose he is to work out the battle of Bunker Hill; to create a full and vivid picture; to note its purpose and results, immediate and remote; to mark its parts, and their relations to each other; or something of this sort. Where is the end to this lesson? This battle may be treated in two paragraphs, which he might commit in half the allotted time. In such a case, he ought to change his work; and the sooner the better. This battle has enough to engage all the power of the historian for thirty minutes or thirty days. Why not put it to the class so that the strongest might exhaust his time and strength, and yet the weakest have something he can profitably do?

It is easy for a pupil to persuade himself that he has his lesson, and dangerous to indulge him in that direction. What he needs, more than history, is power to fasten his thought on a given problem. The strict requirements of the study period should confer this power. One of the best disciplinary opportunities in the school is just this furnished by the study time, in which the teacher can help the pupil to hold himself continuously to one object of thought. His untrained mind moves to its work confusedly, and leaps from one thing to another without method and continuity. The strict requirement of unity is essential, not only in learning the assigned lesson, but to the more valuable end of continued and concentrated attention on whatever he undertakes to master. To keep interesting story books on the teacher's desk, that a pupil may interest and busy himself after he thinks he has done his lesson, while better than flogging for mischief, does not favor order and good discipline. This indulges his caprice, and encourages him to persuade himself that he knows what he does not know, and defeats discipline in power of concentration and continued effort; certainly a quality as much to be desired as the knowledge to be gained in the study period.

No; the more one thinks of it, so far as the lower grades of school are concerned, the more rigid does the law appear that the pupil must not change his subject of study during the programmed time for class-study. When such a requirement becomes useless to him, he no longer needs to study under the immediate direction of the teacher. Let it be concluded, therefore, that, unless the house is on fire, pupils in the class studying must stick, without wavering, to the question set for that time.

Unity in Class Reciting. — The ideal to be secured in the class reciting is, that all pupils fuse with the teacher in an unbroken effort to grasp the problem under consideration. Again, let us insist that the unity of one pupil with another — a mere external unity — is not the unity desired. Such a unity will be secured as a result of the essential unity of pupils with teacher. The skill of the teacher in the recitation will be summed up in the degree of undivided effort secured. The greater the amount and intensity of mental activity aroused in conjunction with the thought of the teacher, the higher should be our estimate of the teaching skill.

1. The first point to receive attention here is the same as that already discussed for securing attention in the class studying, — namely, the comfortable, buoyant, and spirited condition of pupils; and since, if more than one class, the recitation and the study begin practically together, the conditions are secured at the same time.

2. The other general condition essential to unity is that of thorough preparation on the part of both teacher and pupil. On the part of the pupil, this has been provided for in the study hour. No source of failure is so

fruitful as the lack of preparation of the lesson by the teacher. The teacher must have so mastered the lesson that he feels his freedom in the thought to be presented. Vague and partial knowledge cannot guide and strengthen. The thought of the lesson must have been so mastered that the teacher will feel perfectly at home in whatever new and unexpected turn the discussion may take; and such turn it is sure to take.

The lesson must be thoroughly prepared, not only to enable the teacher to guide with steady hand the various activities of the pupils to the end sought, but also to draw all to himself by the law of unconscious sympathy. A teacher has no right to hear a lesson until he has become inspired through a deep study of it; and then, approaching the class filled and thrilled with his message, the pupils unconsciously bend forward, and are fused into one by the heat of his thought. Skill in teaching can never be cold and mechanical. Whatever the thought to be presented, it must be so wrought into the teacher's being, that it will glow with warmth of life. And note that this is not merely an interest in the matter of the lesson, but an interest in the result to be produced in the pupil by means of the lesson. The preparation of the lesson is the study of the matter in relation to the life of the pupil. The teacher's problem is, "What change can I make in the pupil's life by the means now at my command?" This problem thoroughly entered into, and the teacher becomes burdened with a message to his pupils. Seeing clearly his means, and feeling deeply his opportunity, he approaches his class with that flush and glow of interest which kindles the thought and warms the heart of those he instructs. It is all a question of downright earnestness and sincerity of purpose; a burning desire to quicken the soul of the child into the highest good of life.

3. The next step is to secure the outer form of unity, and the attitude of attention. The desks should be cleared of everything not needed in the recitation. The class should be seated in a compact form; and all lines straight from front to back, and from right to left. There should be no vacant place within the compass of the class. The class should look well as a body. The teacher cannot think straight in the presence of a crooked and ragged form. The question often arises: "Ought classes to recite in their study forms, or be called to recitation seats?" This cannot be answered till all the conditions are given. The place should be chosen which will best secure unity under the conditions. The question of removing the class to prevent disturbance of others is a determining factor. The ideal is a neatly and compactly formed class, removed, if necessary, so as not to disturb, or be disturbed by, others. Now, with the eyes of the pupils fixed on the teacher, in obedience to some noiseless signal, all are ready for the thought movement of the lesson.

4. The thought of the class will move forward by means of directions, questions, and explanations or lectures.

Directions. — In giving directions, the golden rule is

to give the direction so that all pupils will do the same thing at the same time. There may be exceptions — but they are rare — permitting one part of the class to do one thing, while others are differently engaged. Nothing, for example, could be more inartistic and less effective than to announce in turn different sentences for the members of the class to pass to the board and diagram. Each one is concerned with his own little affair, and as soon as a pupil has written his sentence he may turn his thoughts to mischief, or prop himself up against the wall, waiting patiently for his slow turn. Without passing to the board, wasting time and chalk, all minds might be riveted on the same thought concerning the sentence, allowing no time for dozing or dissipation. Thus each pupil is required to put forth his most intense activity for the entire time, avoiding the half-asleep kind of thinking so fatal to intellectual life. This, however, according to some theories, may be all wrong, as it interferes with the pupil's freedom and individuality.

Here is a picture taken from life: School-room of two grades (seventh and eighth), of about twenty pupils each. Good teacher, as the world goes; lesson in denominate numbers by the seventh grade. Teacher directs one boy to pass to the board and solve the first problem; another, the second; and so on till the ten problems are used. Then, commencing again with the first problem, re-assigns the ten problems severally to the next ten pupils. A few pupils still remain without work, and these are given selected problems to work at desks, the board all being occupied. The teacher now steps back to talk to the visitor while waiting developments. Things always develop rapidly under such circumstances; and soon the teacher is needed by a girl working at her desk, where teacher and pupil discuss the problem. Note here that it is all right for teacher and pupil to talk during recitation, because the teacher makes the rules: two pupils must not talk; except to help each other, as they say. And this they soon do, for the bright girl points the way to the dull boy. The first boy has done his sum; and, rather than waste time, punches the fire, which is already too hot. Another bright lad cultivates the fantasy and freehand drawing; while some laggards toil on, with and without help, hopeless, and despairing of victory before time is called. The first boy explains to those who have done their work, while others toil on. Fill out the picture at your leisure. In all it was a splendid display of self-activity, free thought, and free speech.

What would that teacher have gained if he had required all the problems to be put in neat form of process on slates or note books; so that at the recitation he might have done something like this: Called on the class as a whole for the first step in the problem, permitting one to speak for the class; then have said, "Take the step," calling on one to speak for the class again. And thus moving rapidly till all problems were solved. With pupils neat, prim, and orderly in their desks, each pupil might have been compelled to think each problem through, and so have multiplied immeasurably the amount and intensity

10

of thought for the given time.   The recitation is not the time to wait for a pupil to solve a problem.   All must be ready to pull together, and the teacher must see to it that the highest combined energy of thought is secured.

Such recitations as the above do not only require no effort in recitation, but require no effort in preparation. Each pupil, knowing that he has but one problem to solve, is apt to take his chances without definite preparation. He will read the first problem, and decide that he can solve it on the spur of the moment.   If he finds one that is peculiarly difficult, he knows that twenty chances to one it will come to some one else.   If he is a farmer's boy, and trained to bind wheat all day under a scorching sun, he may know no better than to work away with all his might; but such industry does not come from the teaching.

Questions. — This is a unique method of instruction, based on the assumption that knowledge is born in the mind, — is of the mind, and not something to be put into it from the outside.   Teaching by giving directions partakes somewhat of the same nature, but not so exclusively. The question is a clear recognition of the fact that knowledge is a process in the mind of the learner, — a favorite doctrine of Socrates, on which was based the Socratic question.   The chief merit in his method of instruction was not so much in the fact that he used an ingenious form of questioning, as in the due recognition of self-activity in the process of learning.   With him instruction could not deliver ideas by conveyance from one to another, but must stimulate self-activity into processes of knowledge. The new education dates back at least to Socrates.

In thus stimulating self-activity the questioning of Socrates took a surprising turn. Usually questions are asked to obtain information. The one addressed is assumed to know the answer, while the questioner is supposed to be ignorant of it. When you ask a man the way to town, he is supposed to know, but you are not. On any other assumption he would ordinarily feel that your question is impertinent. The vexing thing about the questioning of Socrates was the fact that he asked questions of people not supposed to know the answer; and not for the purpose of gaining information, as he ironically pretended to do. People were not used to such impertinence, and sometimes talked angrily to Socrates, and refused to answer his ironical questions; which, while bringing Socrates no information, made other people so unpleasantly conscious of ignorance. After all that has been said about the Socratic question, I suppose the unique thing about it was the reversal of the ordinary movement of thought in a question. The Socratic question is simply the teaching question. His exceptional skill in the use of it could not have given rise to a distinct species of questioning. He may have made excessive use of pretence to be asking questions in the customary way; hence the ironical feature; but the chief point is the use of the question in teaching as different from that in gaining information.

The foregoing suggests the true nature and principle of

questioning. The question causes a tension between the mind and an object, and challenges the mind to cancel the tension. The mind, quiescent, is made conscious of ignorance; then the tension arises, which tends to release itself in knowledge. The teaching question makes the mind conscious of limitation, but requires the removal of limitation in the acquisition of knowledge. Thus it is clear that that question is best which sets up the strongest tension between the mind and the unknown object. The differences in the art of questioning are finally tested at this point; and if the teacher will recall his experience in questioning, he will discover that his effort and his difficulty have been to secure the required stress on the part of the pupil. The law, therefore, requires that the question secure the highest possible tension of thought on the point under discussion; that it be put so that the pupil must think; not dream, guess, or answer automatically.

Turning now to questioning classes, the law must have an additional emphasis, — that of forcing every member of the class to think the answer.

This is the fundamental truth in all directions as to how, and how not, to question. For instance, it is properly said that the question should be asked before designating the one to answer. If the teacher should say, "John, you may stand now; I wish to ask you a question. Which is the longest river in the world?" the other members of the class are excused, and each may engage in his own line of thought. But if the teacher should say, "Which is the longest river in the world?" and then, after a short pause, and without any indication as to whom the question would fall, say, "John," all must have thought the answer in expectation of giving it. No matter if only one has answered, all have recited. It is said that a teacher should not call on pupils in regular order. This follows from the fact that a pupil may anticipate his question, and withdraw from the line of thought till his turn comes. A teacher should not indicate, by naming, by gesture, by look, or by regular order of procedure, the one who is to answer until all are thinking the answer.

We are told not to ask questions which can be answered by yes or no. Such questions can be answered without thinking; and pupils say yes and no automatically, while thinking of things other than the subject under consideration. Such questions are easy to ask; and, since in one chance out of two the pupil hits the perfect answer, many fall into this loose form of questioning.

Verbose questioning is a serious and common error against unity. "Now, Mary, I wish, if you please, you would answer me this question: Who is the author of 'Snow Bound'?" All of this, except the question, is not only useless, but dissipates the energy of the class by not giving them something to do. Still better to put it in this form: "Author of 'Snow Bound'?" This is quickly done, and perfectly clear. Many such can be dropped out and answered, while a single one, like the first, would drag its slow length along. As a rule, one-half the words used by the teacher may be omitted, and the effect multiplied. We like to hear ourselves talk, and keep the air rolling with sound, thinking that there must be highly charged thought with so much rumbling noise. A passenger at the Terre Haute station says to the agent: "Good-morning, sir. Can you wait on me now? Will you please give me a ticket to Indianapolis?" Why not say, "A ticket to Indianapolis"? Better this: "To Indianapolis." Best this: "Indianapolis." It will be perfectly clear, if the word is accompanied with a five dollar bill; and, besides, the passenger may hope to take the first train. So in teaching: the polite, formal, and verbose deliverance may often be reduced to a monosyllable, and avoid leaving passengers behind the train of thought.

Explanations or Lectures. — In giving pupils directions, or in asking them questions, they are supposed to be able to put things together, and to reach conclusions themselves; and these methods put the subject-matter before pupils so as to stimulate them to make such original constructions. There may arise conditions which require the teacher to give aid in explanations, and sometimes, in the more formal lecture. This method assumes that pupils have already arrived at an active, anxious state of mind touching the subject of discussion. If pupils are indifferent, or relaxed in mental attitude, talk will not reach them; they themselves must be put to work on the problem. Students know well how easy it is to take a course by lectures in university work; and even the best student will relax his effort when put in the receptive rather than in the constructive attitude. The lecture method is an excellent one for the professor; for he must thus initiate, construct, and investigate systems of thought. The value of this to himself ought to convince him that it would be best to direct the student to original investigations and constructions, and require the student to deliver the lecture to the patient and long-suffering professor, rather than cultivate such virtues in the student.

Yet the teacher must explain, and sometimes lecture; but this must be done warily, because the pupil so easily relaxes mental energy when the teacher assumes the responsibility. Such method is needed and proper only when pupils are brought to such firm tension with their subject that no risk of relaxation is assumed. Only then will talk from the teacher reach its aim. There are classes and audiences in such attitude as not only to justify, but to require, continued discourse from the instructor. Such method, when the conditions permit, secures rapidity in development of thought. Development by directions and questions is a tedious process; and when the teacher is sure that the development will go on in the pupil's mind by merely listening to discourse, he should use the more expeditious method. So that the lecture method, like any other method, cannot be praised or blamed in itself; it is all a question of adaptation to known conditions in the mind of the learner. While its use is most efficient when the conditions justify, it can be rarely justified; and as rarely in the university as in the kindergarten. So rare indeed is its proper use, that the ideal of the teacher should be that of keeping as nearly silent as possible during the recitation. No fault of the recitation is more obstrusive than that of too much talk from the teacher. The beautiful recitation is marked by the quietness and seeming lack of effort on the part of the teacher, accompanied by mental strain and stress on the part of pupils. The recitation is for the sake of the pupil's effort and not the teacher's; and whatever display of energy there may be must come from them and not from him. Quite often the brilliant performance of the teacher in the recitation puts under suspicion the value of his work to the class. The artistic teacher will obscure himself as much as possible, and make as prominent as possible the effort and products of his pupils. Anything else, since the class is the end and the teacher the means, is distortion.

Obstacles in Forward Movement. — A chief obstacle in maintaining the movement of the class in unity is that of diverse ability in its membership, and the necessity of helping the weak pupil. The temptation in such cases is to give personal help; and the question often arises as to how far the giving of special help is permissible during the recitation period. In this matter the principle of unity is the sufficient guide. We have seen that in the very nature of class work it is all individual help; but that it must always be the help of all. This principle of helping all in every act of instruction must not be violated; but its application is so elastic as to permit much aid to the weak pupil while continuing the activity of the strong.

Suppose a pupil fails to follow the development of an idea in class, the teacher must begin at the first and redevelop with the whole class. This process may be repeated up to the point of risk in losing attention of other members of the class through a sense of familiarity and useless repetition. It is always probable that a considerable repetition of the process is good for all; but when it passes this point, the weak pupil must secure the services of the teacher out of session hours. Instead of keeping the pupil in, it seems much nicer to the pupil to keep the teacher in; and if the teacher understands his relation to the pupil, and desires a quiet and a happy household, he will ingeniously and cheerfully shift requirement and responsibility of keeping in after school to the side of the pupil. A cheerful offering of service after school hours, when the pupil has been made to feel the need of that service, releases the teacher from further responsibility. At any rate, if the pupil does not feel the need of the assistance and thus desire it, the friction caused by his forcible detention renders useless the service of the teacher after school hours.

In the process of recitation, the teacher must avoid thrusting anything between the thought on the point under discussion and the minds of the class. A prominent form of this is that of requiring pupils to recite in words of the text, as if the text were a collection of memory gems. The recitation is a movement of thought on a given theme, and whatever requires straining to conform to language, when the form of language is not essential, checks the free movement of thought. The *memoriter* recitation may be very beautiful in outer form, but, closely inspected, it reveals distortion. The pride of the teacher in the prim and so-called perfect recitation leads to formal and mechanical work, which defeats the object of the recitation. This prevails to such an extent that it is well to beware of the pretty and perfect recitation.

When a history class, seated ever so correctly, with arms folded, say off in order, each in turn, the paragraphs of the lesson, and repeat by ingenious distribution till all show perfect preparation, it is not beautiful, because not the freedom of the inner life. Yet teachers have commanded exceptional salaries for skill in neat, ingenious mechanism. Two kinds of recitation in geometry are often heard. In one each member moves through the demonstration without a halt, and triumphantly; following the figures and letters precisely as given in the text. In the other, the members struggle, stumble, and fail in the effort at original demonstration; but in this case there is intense and free demonstrative activity, while in the former there is but the pretence of demonstration ingeniously obscured by the perfect form of it. The recitation is beautiful just in proportion as it secures energy of thought, however struggling and halting it may seem; and the beautiful external form may be secured at the expense of this. The neat, prim form of recitation is to be desired; all things should be done decently and in order; but the beauty of form should be discriminated from the beauty of life, and not permitted to crush out the life it is to serve.

Another very effective method of shackling the movement of thought, is that of constraining pupils to think
and express in conformity with the teacher's thought and
expression.   This is a most subtle form of the cramming
process, and practiced much by those who condemn that
process.   They would not for the world force pupils to
the acceptance of ready-made products of the text; but
they manage to bring pupils around exactly to their own
forms and conclusions.

The guessing, or developing, lesson is a very popular
mode of obstructing the free movement of thought.   We
are told that we must not tell the pupil anything which
he can find out for himself; and straightway we infer that
he can find out everything, and that it must be developed
out of him.   Often when we think such has been accomplished, it comes either from a sly hint from the teacher,
or from a statement of a member of the class.   In most
cases when a class throw up hands, and the teacher
exclaims, "Behold it has been developed!" it has only
been surmised and guessed at by many wasteful efforts.
The time wasted in the over-developing process is alarming.   When the teacher knows that he must virtually give
the point to the class, as will often happen, he should do
so at once; and not stop to practice developing, and to play
with his art.   Guessing lessons are not thinking lessons;
and the pupil ought never to be put in the attitude of guessing at what is in the teacher's mind.

Again, to sit with class-book and pencil, noting the
exact weight of the thought delivered, in pwt. and gr., is

fatal to the fullest and freest activity on the part of the pupil; and, for that matter, the teacher also. Especially is this objectionable when the teacher threatens the pupil with his poor marking. "There goes another zero for you; you will have this work all to do over if you do not begin to make a better record soon." This leads me to speak more broadly of the law of sympathy between teacher and pupil as the great secret of unity between the two.

Unity is mainly secured by the law of sympathy between the mind of the teacher and the pupil in the activity of thought. It has already been noted that the teacher should become inspired with the lesson before attempting to hear it; and when the recitation comes, the class will be unconsciously drawn into his thought, and without conscious means on the part of the teacher. What I wish especially to emphasize here is that the teacher must not, by personal attack of any kind, interrupt the flow of good feeling between himself and pupils. While warmly personal, the teacher must be impersonal. There must be no personal conflict. Suppose the boy fails to recite, the teacher should not say: "You have been trifling your time away; I heard you were loafing last night instead of getting your lesson. You will have to do this work all over, if you do not mend your ways." I know of no circumstances under which a pupil should be berated in the presence of the class. He must be treated politely, — that is, as if he were an ideal student. Teachers often complain of the impoliteness of pupils; but teachers are much more frequently guilty of this offence. Personal reproof in class is a most common practice, from the primary grades through the college. The pupil who does poorly should be privately interviewed by the teacher; and then the case should be approached with sympathy, as if there were some reason for the poor preparation, — bad health, too much work to do, visit from distant relative, etc. It is easy to make a grave blunder by off-hand charges. It is safest at the time to suppose that the failure is excusable, and then privately press it to the real reason, commencing with excusable ones.

So far the attempt has been to illustrate the doctrine of unity in school-management, when all minds are favorably disposed. Through ignorance, thoughtlessness, or wilfulness, unity may be broken; it must then be restored. This brings us to the delicate and important question: —

Restoration of Broken Unity.

This topic has, in general, the same significance as that of correction, or punishment; but the wording is preferable, especially to that of punishment, because it does not convey so prominently the idea of inflicting pain, which is not essential to restoration of unity. We need first to search out, in light of the law of unity: —

The Law of Restoration. — This must be found in the spiritual unity of the organism; for it is this, and not the external form of unity, that is to be restored. When pupils bolt the recitation, the material and external side of the unity is broken; but this is only the result of the broken spiritual unity. What the law requires is not a spatial unity, nor even a unity of forced consent; but the cheerful purposed co-operation of pupils with teacher.

We are so accustomed to think of this matter under the name and law of punishment, that it may be most easily approached from that standpoint. When rightly interpreted, the law of punishment is well stated in saying: *Punishment must naturally follow the offence, and be proportioned to it.* This has, however, been most viciously applied. Suppose a boy has played truant a quarter of a day; then, by the nature of the offence, it is thought he should remain in after school to make up lost time. And to make it mathematically proportionate, he should remain in just the length of time lost. The girl whispers, and thus annoys the teacher; it is but just that she be equally annoyed by the teacher. One boy blacks the eye of another; and, in turn, he must be bruised in equal area. An eye for an eye, and a tooth for a tooth. Pupils show that they understand this mathematical system of justice by insisting that the same number of lashes should follow the same offence. When offences are equal, it would not do for the teacher to give one boy four lashes and the other five.

This idea of the law above stated must be put aside as a dangerous one. The thought of getting even with the offender must never guide the teacher. Retribution must have no place in punishment. It is external means applied to the external side of the offence; it can never reach the offence, but always aggravates it. During the trials and worry of the day the teacher is in a mood to "pay up" for everything that annoys him; but he must crush every suggestion of the so-called even-handed justice.

Let it not be forgotten that punishment, or correction, is for the purpose of restoring unity, and that the above law is a statement of the means to that end. The trouble in applying the law is in not noting carefully the nature of an offence. The offence is in the will, the choice, of the pupil, and not in his external deed. In itself it is not wrong to stay out of school. If the pupil has the measles, it is even right to remain out. To be absent a week is right, when, by so doing, means are secured to attend school two more weeks than would otherwise be possible. Whispering in itself is not wrong; under certain circumstances it is delightfully proper. A pupil may whistle in the bounds of duty and propriety; there is no offence in the nature of the act as such. It is only when the pupil, by such means, consents to break the unity of the school that his act becomes an offence. The offence is in the intention. His deed is in his mind. A wrong act, or an offence, is a choice against the spiritual unity of the school. The pupil may remain out of school entirely against his will; then he is spiritually at one with the school. Though absent in body, he is present in mind. Were he present in body by force, willing to be elsewhere, he would still be an offender. The pupil who wills to remain out of school has done that which, if generalized, would destroy the organization, and thus defeat its purpose. An offence in school is always a choice in a line of action which will destroy, or tend to destroy, the school. The end of the school cannot be attained if whispering be chosen as a practice. The pupil who whispers, in a way, consents to that which tends to defeat the purpose of the school. The offence is in his mind, and not in his outer deed. And this offence does not consist in the mere fact of consenting to whisper in school. One may whisper in school or other organized body with perfect propriety. Suppose a political speaker or a minister in his sermon makes a good hit, an auditor might well nudge his neighbor and whisper, "That's good, that's good!" And when the fervor of the occasion waxes warm the shout of an "Amen" might further the interests of the occasion. The evil lies only in the consent to do that kind of whispering which if generalized would defeat, or tend to defeat, the purpose of the organization. It is that whispering which one would desire to conceal from the will of the organization as embodied in the ruling officer; it is that consent which has its universal setting in a disposition to destroy the organization of which the individual is a part, and for whose good the organization exists.

Let this distinction be clearly impressed; for a failure to distinguish between the pupil's outer deed and his inner spirit is a fruitful source of bad management. The pupil must purpose, must will, in harmony with the end of the school of which he is a part. It is a spiritual unity. The pupil is a spiritual member. and is in the

spiritual unity, when he desires and purposes the good of
the whole.   He spiritually severs his connection with the
school when he gives his mind to that which disintegrates
the school.   It thus appears that a pupil, and the pupil
alone, has the power to sever his connection with the
school.   In the best sense, he alone can suspend himself.
Wycliffe said that you cannot excommunicate a man from
church unless he first excommunicate himself.   That is,
if a man is a true Christian, and the church vote him out,
he is not out, but the church is out; and if he is a bad
man, and the church still claim him, he and they are
both out.

An offence, then, is the action of the will, on the part
of either pupil or teacher, which negatives the will creating
and sustaining the school, — the will as embodied in, and
interpreted by, the teacher and school officers.   It is the
individual's purpose set counter to the whole.   This makes
the application of the law clear.   If correction, or punishment, naturally follows the offence, it is by an action of
the will in the offender; and if it be proportioned to the
offence, it must completely reverse the wrong action of
the will.   The pupil who breaks the spiritual unity of the
school by choosing against it, must reverse that choice
before he has cancelled his offence.   This makes his
punishment follow naturally the offence, and proportions
it to the offence; for he simply undoes his wrong act, and
thereby restores himself to the institution.   The pupil
alone has the power to sever his connection with the
school; and he alone has the power to reinstate himself

11

when once out. No mechanical process can restore the pupil whose mind is at variance with the institution; he must reinstate himself by changing his spiritual attitude.

Thus briefly we have suggested how to restore the unity when broken: *The pupil who breaks the unity must, by his own act of mind, restore it.* And the law of punishment stated at the outset means just this: the deed being in the will, the punishment must be there too; and when the will has cancelled its own deed, the punishment is exactly proportioned to the offence. Anything beyond this is gratuitous on the part of the teacher, and an aggression on the rights of the pupil. The idea of retribution is thus excluded.

School punishment is not the application of external means; it is the struggle the pupil has with himself in order to subordinate himself to the purpose of the school. To bring this struggle to pass is the business of the teacher; knowing, however, that the work is essentially done by the pupil himself. This puts the responsibility where it belongs,— with the wrongdoer. He must wrestle with his own deed. Whatever pain is suggested by the word punishment should be that of mental pain. And there is nothing more severe than for the pupil to bring himself to take his stand against his former action and disposition.

Application of the Law. — The first practical inference from this law of punishment is this: The teacher must at all times conduct himself as if it were the pupil's business to correct his own deed, and not as if it were the teacher's business to adjust the case for him. Teachers talk among themselves, and with pupils, as if it were the teacher's work to adjust the pupil's mischief. If a boy in the high school plays truant, the question is not what the teacher is going to do about it, but what is the boy going to do about it. Pupils sent from the grades to the superintendent for correction suppose that he is to do something with them that will square the account. In such cases the superintendent should be passive, only witnessing what disposition they make of their own deed. He should aid, of course, by whatever suggestions and directions he may find helpful; but the pupil must feel that he alone can make right his own wrong. Nothing done by any one else can reach the case. This does not mean that the teacher is to do nothing, but only suggests the attitude in his doing. Just what he is to do may also be inferred from the nature of a wrong deed.

The pupil, to correct his deed, must see its relation to the school, and then must decide to act in harmony with the school. For the sake of clearness, suppose that a young man in college bolts the recitation. By so doing he has given his consent to break up the institution; for he has done that which, if done by all, would defeat the purpose of the school. His act tends to destroy the organization. Now what is to be done with him? No; what is he to do with himself? He must see the meaning of his act; and, in the light of what he sees, must choose to co-operate to the end for which the school is established. This was his contract when he entered, by the very fact of his entrance.

If he should remain out, the case is settled, for he has a right to withdraw. But if he should present himself for admission, he should be informed that he is no longer a part of the institution. At this point the burden of correction rests with the student. If he manifests a desire to reinstate himself, he should be asked to explain why a pupil should not desert the class. This reason he should work out in a clear, logical, and convincing argument. It could be made a splendid exercise in demonstrative reasoning, and would be more valuable to the young man than to prove the Pythagorean proposition. Suppose he says that he cannot see clearly why a student should not bolt. In this case he should drop his regular studies and become a specialist on the subject of bolting. He should have kind and sympathetic help while struggling out of school with this problem; he should be asked to present his solution as soon as he has it worked out; but he should not, under any consideration, be permitted to work with the school until he is clear on the point of bolting. I do not mean that he should not be permitted to remain in the study room while working out his problem; but that he should not be included with other students in the regular school work. He should not participate in any of the regular school exercises; yet his presence in the school-room, where he can receive suggestions, and so that he will not be delayed in making his report as soon as he has it ready, is desirable. It would be a rash and dangerous mistake to thrust the pupil out of the school-room, proclaiming a suspension or an expulsion. Although the pupil is really out by his own act, he is out of the spiritual unity, and not necessarily out-of-doors. He might, for a time, at least, be entertained as a polite visitor, or assisted as a student taking a special course.

When the young man shows that he sees his duty clearly, that ends the matter, for the present at least. Most cases of disorder arise from lack of clear perception of the pupil's relation to the school; and the teacher must rely on bringing the pupil to a realizing sense of this relation to remedy disorder. Besides, it is unsafe to question the pupil's motive by making further requisition till necessary. To take a step that might not be needed would undo all that had been done, and incite to worse conduct in the future. On second offence, the teacher might remark, "I thought you understood the matter clearly." If he admits that it was not so clear as he had supposed, he must be put to work out his relations to the school as before; but if he proves that he does understand the matter, then the teacher is to take the last step, appealing to the will, and that is to ask him what he is going to do about it. If he says that he does not know, he should be asked to return and report as soon as he has his mind made up. This is a very serious process, and he should be given time to make it up well. But usually the first step is the most difficult. When the nature of the wrong deed is seen clearly, the choice readily follows, except in cases of stubbornness. To awaken thought on the question is usually sufficient to correct the evil; but this is not neces-

sarily so.   The pupil should not be reinstated until he
affirms his intention to do nothing except that which
furthers the work of the school.   Note this: it is not
enough for him to resolve against truancy; he must
resolve to preserve unity.   He might pledge himself
against truancy and have a mental reservation to substitute some other form of evil.   He may thus invent faster
than the teacher can correct.   If pupils flip shot in time
of school, and this particular offence be corrected, they
will surely flip beans next; and this being corrected, they
will at once resort to paper wads; and so on *ad infinitum.*
The correction to be effective must be universal.   The
particular form of evil is a matter of no consequence; we
are concerned only with that disposition in the pupil
which can develop forms of evil infinitely.   The particular
evil which the teacher detects must be taken only as a sign
of a constitutional trouble which must have constitutional
treatment.   This, and not the form of vice, the teacher
must remedy.   And to this end it matters not what form
the offence may take; the teacher must press these two
questions: Do you see?   What are you going to do about
it?   But what if he break his resolution?   This is no
proof that he was insincere in making it.   He should then
repeat his former process.   It may prove finally that he
is not honest in his effort.   Then the way is clear; for he
should have no further opportunity to reinstate himself.
But so long as he is honestly striving, he is gaining
strength, and should not be excluded from school.   It is
not safe to accuse a pupil of falsehood simply because he

fails to carry out his affirmed intention. Much patience must be exercised, and the process with the pupil repeated so long as he is gaining strength thereby; unless the welfare of the school is too much endangered,— the loss to the school greater than the gain to the pupil.

In the foregoing case of correction there is more or less of authority exercised over the student, inasmuch as he is not permitted to choose freely for himself in the matter. A change in this respect takes place in passing from the college to the university student. The university student is supposed to have brought himself under the rule of reason, — to be able to think things under universal relations, and to regulate conduct by universal principles. He practically gives law to the university. He largely determines its general policy, and chooses to do as his own reason may dictate, within the limits of general morality, and his fitness to do certain work, which must be determined by others. But whether the student attend a particular lecture at a particular time on a particular point must be left to him. The teacher holds him only for the general outcome of his work, knowing that the student is able, or should be able, to best guide himself in the details of his progress, free from the minute supervision which must be imposed on the more immature student. The teacher in the university has only to pronounce judgment on the attainment of the student as to the subject in which the teacher gives instruction. What a university student may properly do would not be proper for the kindergarten student, the primary student, or even the high school or college student. External authority decreases in moving upward; the possible points at which law may be violated increase in passing downward. This suggests that one thing ought to be made clear to the student from the beginning, and as rapidly as possible; namely, the reasonableness in obeying authority,— those who interpret and apply the law. And further, the change here indicated in passing from the kindergarten to the university student, ought to suggest to the teacher that, in making corrections, he take the development of the pupil into the account.

The treatment of the college student, as in the case supposed, is somewhat simplified by the fact that he is supposed to be out from under home control. The case of the high school student is different; for parents have something to do in shaping his school conduct. The steps in correction are the same; but there may be cases in which it is necessary for the parent to assist the student to see his relation to the school, and to strengthen his resolution to keep in harmony with the general good. If the young lady whispers, she must first show why such conduct defeats the purpose of the school, and therein is highway robbery of the taxgatherer. If she cannot readily work this problem out, she should drop all other studies until her deficiency is made up. She has really suspended herself; but it is no use to be harsh, and have her pack her books for home. Simply change her work for a more important line of investigation,— for something really practical in life. She may go to church some time, and it will be worth everything to all parties

concerned for her to know the ground of silence in
organized assemblies.   Her religion depends upon it.
The teacher must be patient in giving assistance; and
when he finds that his suggestions may not be sufficient,
he should suggest that she ask for help at home; for
certainly her parents know why silence is the law of the
school.   I am supposing here, for the sake of the illustration, what is not likely to happen; for a high school girl
can easily make clear the law against communication in
school.   A teacher does not yield his authority in bringing
parents into such discussions.   Nothing is lost; everything is gained: a clear, mutual understanding all around,
with the co-operation of the parents.   It is all firm, fair,
calm, and just dealing.   Let us say again to the teacher
that such a course is no condescension from the throne of
authority; for the authority is not in the teacher, but in
the nature of the school and the work to be done.   On the
other hand, the parent has no right to shirk duty, and
inform the teacher that if he cannot manage the school he
had better give way to some one who can.   The pupil is
his child, and he is, in a sense, responsible for her conduct, and should be glad of any opportunity afforded by
the teacher to help form it.

When the reason against communication has been clearly
worked out, then the case may be dismissed as before,
confidently expecting improved conduct in the future.   If
the offence should be repeated, and perception of duty
tested as before, then she is ready for the question,
"What are you going to do about it?"   She may not

know at first; but the teacher must keep cool, and give her time to find out. If she cannot decide to desist from communication, she should not re-enter school. This is suspension by her own act. I have often been asked what the teacher would do if the school board should sustain the pupil. I cannot conceive of such a case. What school board would ever support the student who has taken his stand in favor of any evil line of action? The trouble with the teacher in such cases is that he does not bring the matter to the square issue. Let the teacher ask the pupil in the presence of the board what she intends to do in respect to the matter under question; and in the case supposed the board cannot say, "Let her communicate;" for the fearful results from such an order from the school board would be too obvious to need discussion.

The same steps in punishment for the high school pupil are required for the grade below; the difference is in the manner of treatment. The primary pupil can make clear the reason against all the general forms of bad conduct. Through his instinctive obedience he will do what he thinks the teacher desires; yet the teacher must substitute, as rapidly as possible, rational self-control for natural obedience. Pupils must be led to see why certain conduct is beautiful and good, aside from the will of the teacher, and should be exercised in freedom to follow their own insight into duty as revealed by their relation to work being done.

The most troublesome cases will appear in the intermediate grades. These pupils have passed the stage of natural obedience, and have not yet arrived at rational self-control. They are becoming conscious of will power, and are beginning to assert their individuality against everything else. This is the young American who knows no law but his own caprice. But the process in punishment, except in details, must be the same as before described. He will need more frequent applications of the process, and a more patient working out of details.

The teacher who reads these suggestions must not suppose that the law will apply itself; or that all cases of bad conduct will be satisfactorily reached by it. There may be some cases that nothing will correct; and then, too, there is a world of difference in the tact of the teacher in applying the law. Every case has its peculiarities, and the details of correction must shape themselves in the process of correction. Let the teacher who finds this law to fail him — and there are such — announce the law under which he succeeds.

The two foregoing steps move inevitably either to the correction of the pupil, or to his exclusion from school. The latter end is to be deplored. But what can be done? Is there no third step to apply to those whom moral suasion will not reach? None of universal application. When the pupil's will proves to be firm and resolute against the law and order of the school, nothing but the application of physical force could be suggested,— some way of reaching the mind through the body,— corporal punishment in its various forms. But it is obvious at once that such means applied to a university student would make matters worse;

the college student could not be persuaded thereby; and there is something in the personal pride and dignity of the high school pupil that would resent such treatment. We cannot speak thus positively in passing from the eighth grade downward to the kindergarten; and yet are we not willing to exempt the eighth grade; and perhaps the seventh also ?   And below these would it do at all to apply corporal punishment to the large number of refined, sensitive, and well-meaning children ?

It thus appears that corporal punishment is not a universal mode of correction. No one believes in its general application; and many deny its virtue altogether. Even laws have been passed prohibiting the teacher from laying hands on the pupil by way of punishment. Yet there are those who would not spare the rod, lest they spoil the child. This may be one of those questions which have two sides. Do not those who condemn it altogether do so because it is an improper method for the great mass of students, and only suitable to the exceptional few; and because, moreover, when it might otherwise be proper, it is applied in anger, and so as to injure the body of the pupil? For these reasons it is thought much safer not to use it at all, than to do so indiscriminately; and with the further risk of its being used by the high-tempered and reckless teacher. In this the law forbidding corporal punishment seems well grounded. And yet cannot any one point out in some community a wrong-headed, tough urchin who would not be degraded by chastisement with the rod, and who would be improved thereby, — one who, all par ties would agree, must be managed by such method at the hands of somebody? Are there not pupils whose integument is the only avenue to the mainspring of conduct? Some appeal must be made; and if no other motive to action is available, sensations must be resorted to. This, therefore, is not a new mode of punishment, but only one of the methods of appeal made necessary because of the absence of higher motives to action. The disgrace is not in the fact of such punishment being a painful physical operation,— if so, amputation of a limb would be still more disgraceful, — but in the degradation implied in assuming the absence of anything but animal sensibilities. The pupil must be taken on the plane of his present life, in order to elevate him above his present life. Punishment, as well as instruction, must follow the law of apperception.

The whole question is this: The instincts, passions, and motives of some pupils being as they are, can an effective appeal be made without some form of corporal application? Can any one show that it is improper under all circumstances for a teacher to lay hands on the pupil? Suppose an intoxicated and enraged pupil break boisterously into the school-room and assault a pupil against whom he is enraged, should not the teacher extemporize a police force at once, and exclude him from the room? A teacher can readily imagine a hundred instances in which hands must be laid upon the pupil. All of which may be most improbable, but it serves to prove that the application of physical force is a proper thing in itself. But aside from such special outbreaks, are there not cases now and then among young pupils in which a kindly corporal chastisement might save society from having to inflict more barbarous punishment later in life?

Suppose in all such cases the teacher is forbidden to use physical persuasion : somebody must do it. Society has yet found no way to avoid laying hands on some individuals. However squeamish we may be about the matter, the individual must yet have corporal punishment by some authorized agency of social welfare. The moment a school board forbids the teacher to lay hands on a pupil by way of punishment, the need arises for some one outside the regular teaching force whose duty it is to perform the objectionable task. Just now, in one of our largest cities, the board are being brought to consider the establishment of "parental schools"; where, it is the presumption, the teacher may inflict such punishment as the law permits the parent to inflict. If the board had kept quiet on the question of corporal punishment, trusting to the selection of a proper teaching force as the best means of solution, they would not have been brought to the humorous situation of having to legalize the practice of corporal punishment. And if the board shirk the duty of providing for pupils who must be appealed to on the physical plane, the civil authorities must take care of them. If a boy is not decently switched in school by the teacher, he may have to be indecently cudgelled by the police after expulsion from school. The last thing the public school should permit is the withdrawal or the expulsion of the pupil from school. The welfare of society requires that all children should have a public school education. Along with the spread of the doctrine of compulsory education — the logical conclusion from the doctrine of a free public school supported by the taxation of all — must follow the corollary requiring that some means be provided to the fullest extent possible for holding the badly-behaved element in school as long as possible, whoever may have to discharge the police duty.

But if the law and the sentiment against corporal punishment are not wholly correct, they will serve to correct the outrageous abuses of the once prevailing system by limiting corporal punishment to the exceptionally few cases to which at most it is applicable; and by causing teachers to be more artful and patient in the use of the proper and universal methods of reform. In fact a teacher should not expect to use corporal punishment,— should even be resolved not to do so, if you wish, — but that he may render the most efficient disciplinary service, no school board should tie his hands by publicly forbidding its use.

The application of the law of unity to punishment carries with it many vital consequences. In the effort to restore unity through punishment, the teacher too often widens the chasm. This arises from the fact that he bears himself as if he were the law of the school. He is the author and executor of the law; whereas the law is inherent in the school, and he, as well as the pupil, is amenable to that law. The procedure which has been suggested would force on the attention of the pupil the fact that the law of the school is given in the purpose and nature of the school, and that neither teacher nor board can legislate beyond the law imposed by the end sought. The pupil must feel that the teacher regards matters thus, and not that his personality is set against that of the pupil. The teacher must step aside and let the pupil wrestle with the law which he himself expounds as arising from the work to be done in the school.

Many of the serious difficulties of management arise from the bearing and words of the teacher, which proclaim that he is "boss" of the institution, and has the power in his right arm to quell any riot that may occur. This attitude will always break the fundamental unity, — the unity between teacher and pupils. The two parties thus formed each strive with the other for the mastery; and from the larger number and the industrious ingenuity on the part of the pupils, it is no wonder that the teacher is so often out-generaled. If it is a personal fight, why not? If the teacher would keep his personality out of the question, and aid the pupil to interpret and apply the law to which both must render obedience, the pupil could not but admire the dignity and firm justice of the system, and esteem the teacher who so patiently and emphatically aids him to see the ground of the law, and to render obedience thereto. There is no reason why a teacher who has common sense and sympathy, and who proceeds in a business-like way in correcting the evil-doer, should drive the pupil from him.

Such a procedure would correct the false sense of honor among pupils, of which we hear so much. A pupil will generally screen his fellow and baffle the teacher in pursuit of an evil-doer. I find that teachers generally consider this honorable conduct on the part of the pupil; and as things are, I suppose it is so. When the teacher sets his personality against the school, who blames the pupil for standing by his friend as against another person? When the teacher asks him to bear witness against a pupil in favor of order, he refuses to do so, feeling that his first duty is to his boon companion. Teachers claim that it is not right for a teacher to ask a pupil to report the bad conduct of another; and they must claim this on the ground that such a course violates the pupil's proper and strong attachment to his fellow-pupil, to serve the teacher's personal gain. The teacher has inculcated the thought that the school is his school; and the pupils properly think, "Let him take care of it; we shall not help him to manage us." If the pupils feel that it is their school, and that the teacher is simply to help them to make it beautiful and good, the sentiment of honor would change from the feeling of honorable conduct towards a comrade as against a teacher, to that of honorable conduct towards the school which is for the good of all his comrades.

Now it is not only proper but obligatory on a pupil to report anything that tends to destroy the successful work· ing of the school. Courts of justice act on this assumption, and imprison the man refusing to give the information. If a pupil should see a stranger set fire to the school building, the fact would instantly be proclaimed; and the same would be expected should the incendiary be a friend of the pupil   He would certainly deny the incendiary to be his friend.   What is the difference between the pupil's setting fire to the building, and doing anything else that would defeat the purpose of the school?   A pupil cannot wilfully screen any wrong-doer without taking his stand against the essential law of the school.   It is a choice to favor the one against the whole number constituting the school, and not against the arbitrary will of the teacher. No, it does not encourage tattling, for tattling has malice in it.   I do not mean that, as a rule, the teacher should use this method of finding out what is going on, but wish to emphasize the relation that should exist between the teacher and the pupil.   They should be in such close partnership, and on such good terms and fair understanding with each other, that the teacher can get whatever it is necessary for him to know.   He should not embarrass pupils by asking for evidence, unless it is absolutely essential; nor should a pupil be made to feel that it is his business to inspect other pupils' conduct, having enough to do to attend to his own.   The teacher himself ought not to assume the function of a spy; he should mingle with pupils in an open and business-like way, and not be continually exercising his authority miscellaneously.   For instance, it is not proper, in meeting a pupil on the street, to assail him with questions of conduct, even though the pupil may then be playing truant.   At such times the pupil must be met on the social plane, and the conversation should run on general matters of the pupil's interest.

The teacher should always mingle with pupils on the

plane of polite society, and when more rugged duties come, let there be a time and place where matters are disposed of in a business-like way.

It is often urged that a pupil should receive his corporal punishment before the school, to deter others from offence. This is vicious doctrine. If corporal punishment is ever proper, it should be given in secret. The teacher then maintains the bond of respect between himself and the pupil, because the pupil's personality is respected in the punishment.

Another vital consequence of the application of the law of unity to punishment is the relief from the worry and nervous strain of the teacher. The teacher, instead of putting himself in conflict with the pupil, puts the pupil in conflict with himself. The pupil cannot be helped except by self-conflict; and the teacher who assumes the pupil's trouble breaks his own nerve, and defeats moral discipline in the pupil. The principle of correction insisted on throughout requires the teacher to fix it up so that the pupil must wrestle with his own deed. This requires skill and ingenuity, but no more worry than the performance of any other duty or the solution of any other difficult problem. It must not be understood that the teacher is to take indifferent ease in the matter, — not at all: it requires patience, careful study, and wise generalship; but this is not worry and vexation at wrong-doing. Can there be any reason why a patient, faithful, conscientious teacher should have the dear life worried out of him by a saucy boy or girl? Why should a teacher who is faithful not be happy, instead of fretting himself because of evil-doers? No, it must be fixed so that the pupil wrestle with his own deed. Remember the advice which one guest gave to another who broke the quiet of the night by walking the floor because his debt was due on the morrow without a cent for payment: "Go to bed and let the other fellow walk the floor!" So should the teacher shape up business that he may go to bed and let the other fellow walk the floor.

Rather than worry, is there not some reason for rejoicing in finding evil manifested? Suppose the boy desire to cut the desk, should not the teacher be pleased that the symptom should appear? If the cut is in the boy, let it come out, that he may be helped to face his deed now, and escape being a vandal when grown up. Let the teacher, in calm patience and joy of opportunity, give such sympathetic counsel as the pupil may need in making the desk and himself whole. There should be no excitement; the teacher should not throw the pupil and the desk out-of-doors, nor disfigure the body of the pupil as a fair offset to his disfigurement of the desk. There should be no haste; the pupil may well consume a week in home consultation and private meditation between sessions, planning the best solution of the difficulty. And all the time the teacher should rejoice in the purifying turmoil; and sooner or later the desk and the boy are made sound and ready for service. If the boy desires to write his autograph on the floor in ink, the teacher should be pleased to have him do so; the problem of rubbing it off can be made so purifying and tonic to his blood. Such experience in erasing sin ought to be one of the most delightful studies of the teacher. Why should he have to resort to fiction to find types of people whose conscience is wringing a sinful heart, when, with such opportunity, it is his business to conduct the conscience-wringing process.

After what has been said, the teacher must not suppose that the prime art of school management consists in the restoration of broken unity, but rather in preserving the unity intact from the outset. The best government is not that which quells the mob, but that which prevents the occurrence of one. The highest ambition of the teacher must never be to display power and ingenuity in bringing order out of confusion, but in avoiding the confusion by perfect adjustment of conditions and skilful instruction. This is the ounce of prevention once more. Hence the skill in management to which the teacher should aspire is that of rendering skill useless.

This suggests the scientific principle for testing school management, — the test of the beautiful. An object is rated beautiful when the moving energy in it is felt not to be hindered by the object. A train is beautiful when the forward-moving energy is felt not to be in bondage to the train. When a train is felt to be heavily laden, the engine puffing and the wheels slipping, awakening in the observer a consciousness of strain, it is thought to be ugly. Any instrument or organization designed to do a given work, and stored with energy in that direction, is beautiful when the instrument or organization does not limit its own energy. A plant or an animal is beautiful when the vital force is triumphant over bodily organization. The school is animated and moved by a school energy, which, as we have seen, is ultimately located in the pupil. For the school to be beautiful, — well-managed, — this energy must not be in bondage to the organization; but the energy must seem to move freely to the end set up. When there is application of external force, the school energy moving out from its centre in the pupil is felt to be interfered with, and the school said to be ugly. Hence a school is beautiful and well-managed when the external force resident in the teacher, or any other external agent, is not felt as a factor controlling the energy which ought to move freely from its inherent source in the pupil. The right conduct of pupils must seem spontaneous under the vital energy of the school, — a free, joyous manifestation of the learning life of the pupil within the organism. Thus we have clear emphasis of the true point of skill in school management; namely, in securing such conditions, and making instruction so vital that external applications to restore order are rendered unnecessary. Such is the ideal to be sought; but because of weakness in both teacher and pupil, it cannot be realized fully. Hence attention must still be given to restoration of broken unity; which, too, out of relation to school management as a whole, may be reduced to the same laws of the beautiful. And the foregoing discussion on restoration of broken unity is an attempt to so reduce it, in the principle that the pupil moves to self-reformation, with the teacher seemingly aside.

Ethical Training within the Organism.

As already pointed out, the organism has an incidental, special value in ethical training, while accomplishing the work for which it is directly designed. It must not be inferred from this that the organism has other than ethical value. Being designed to stimulate the process of growth in the pupil, the entire work of the school is ethical. While its direct purpose is that of giving instruction, this must be taken to include not only intellectual activities, but emotional and volitional experience as well. When a school is properly organized, the emotions and the will are as systematically exercised as the intellect; and this not by separate purposes and processes, but by the organic nature of the teaching act. The term instruction covers the systematic exercise of all the powers; and not by different methods, for by virtue of the unity of the mind and of the subject-matter, all activities are but phases of one life movement for which the school is organized; which movement, taken as a whole, being by tension between the lower and the higher self, is ethical.

But the organism has an inherent secondary ethical value in the process of accomplishing the end for which it is primarily designed. Unlike most other agencies, the material worked upon is a part of the agency. While being taught by the school, the pupil is a part of the school. The pupil is educated through his environment; and the school instituted to do this work becomes at once an immediate and influential part of that environment. So that while the school is organized to give instruction in the broadest sense, it is no sooner put in operation than there appears an ethical value inherent in the life of the organism as such. According to the superficial view, economy requires that all the teacher's effort should be devoted to instruction, feeling that energy expended on management, in order to give instruction, is wasted. Better considered, school management, as a means of cultivating ethical virtues, is worth all the time and energy it costs. The process of managing must be grasped with that of instruction into a total process of reaching the final end in character, and must not be slighted by the feeling that it simply conditions instruction. It is a question of getting the total value out of the organism; and this must include the ethical training involved in the inner working of the organism, as well as the good it objectively seeks.

We must not suppose, however, that there are two kinds of management, — one to secure instruction, with another to secure ethical training. Since all things done right are in fundamental harmony, what is best for instruction is most efficient in ethical training. This harmony of ends at once appears on recalling the fact that the school organization is based in the unity of the pupil's present and future self, and that instruction is also based in the same unity. The organism through instruction brings the pupil into unity with his better self; and the pupil's experience within the organism as such — his experience incident to school organization — must be an experience of unity with his better self. This is the law of unity reappearing in a new form, as: —

Harmony of Means and End. — There must be no conflict beween the end sought by instruction through the organism, and the result of experience in the organism as such. The organism must not contradict itself, — must be in unity with itself in all its influences to the supreme end sought. The purity and integrity of the organism must be maintained in the interest of wholesome school experience, as against any undue pressure in the interest of mere instruction.

Instruction being the primary purpose of the organism, flagrant violations of this law are often committed under the stress of making instruction effective, especially when the true spirit of instruction is wanting. For instance, to force to the highest effort in learning, appeal is quite generally made to the pressure of the per cent system. Admitting for the moment that this end can thus be accomplished, it is obvious that such a course subverts the ethical life of the pupil. The ultimate law of ethics requires that self-activity should not contradict itself; should not play false with itself; that positively it should be consistent with itself. When some artificial stimulus is substituted for the natural tension of thought which the subject, if properly adjusted, will adequately set up, the pupil is caused to practice deceit with his own process of thought. Improper relations to problems of thought are just as immoral as improper relations to one's fellows, and for the same reason; for in both there is breach of integrity in the life process. When a pupil works for per cents he is working for selfish ends, and not for a disinterested object which only can have his true self in it. Just in proportion as a pupil becomes self-conscious through the stimulus of per cents — becomes interested in per cents instead of his subject — to that extent he is in an immoral state of mind.

The use of such means necessarily kills the desire to know; which is immoral because killing the soul itself. When a teacher, in good faith that the natural process of learning is its own sufficient reward, begins to instruct pupils who have been under the artificial stimulus of the per cent system, he finds them to be indifferent to legitimate appeals, and ready to affirm that school life is not worth living without the usual excitement and strife for per cents. What hope for such pupils after the days of formal instruction! The severest criticism that can be made on school work is to show that students after graduation have not a burning desire to pursue a systematic course of study and improvement. The use of false incentives is not the only reason for this; but it is largely chargeable to formal methods of instruction which necessitate artificial incentives, which further render instruction dead and formal. By this process the pupil, if not becoming positively averse to study, feels satisfied and self-sufficient; and having no foreign incentive now offered, he is under no compulsion to further labor. If study means

a contest with ponderable, percentable packages of knowledge, how play the game when there is no one to estimate
and umpire? If the school is to determine to a future
life of study, the motives appealed to and cultivated in
school must be the same as those employed in the natural,
healthful course of life out of school.

And, furthermore, instruction, while supposed to require
the percenting system, prohibits the use of that system as
positively as does the ethical law inherent in the organism.
The intrusion of a foreign element between the pupil and
the object of his thought not only perverts his ethical
relation to the subject he studies, but is an outrage on the
learning process itself. The mind learns by direct tension
with the subject, and insulating non-conductors are fatal
to the process. The use of per cents as a means of instruction shows either that the teacher has no faith in the
passion of the mind for knowledge, and in the power of
the subject to gratify such passion; or it is a confession of
lack of skill in so adjusting one to the other as to utilize
the natural and most powerful motive in study. When
teaching is poorest, the need for per cents is felt to be
greatest, and the most thoroughly and damagingly are
they used. It is not at all strange that, in the childhood
of the profession, before the teacher had found the centre
of his sphere in the unity of pupil and subject-matter,
he should resort to mechanical leverage to force the instruction which his crude art could not otherwise secure.
Nothing to this end has seemed so practical and powerful
as the per cent system; and so universally and thoroughly

has it been used, that it has assumed the rôle of a legitimate and necessary function. Let those who think that
pupils must have other motives to study than the desire
to learn, observe the zest with which the unperverted
and wisely guided kindergarten or primary pupil labors.
Observation proves that the argument for the use of artificial incentives has no force except in case of perverted
appetite for knowledge; and certainly one should not wish
to argue for the continuance of the system which so
perverted the appetite as to make the system necessary.
Even after suffering long abuse of the system, let the
mind of the pupil be brought into living touch with the
thing he studies, and there is instant regeneration, and
bounding forth with alacrity to further explorations. No,
it is faith in the exhilarating touch of the mind with
living truth that saves both teacher and pupil from the
quackery of superficial and temporizing devices as against
natural and constitutional procedure.

The foregoing criticism does not apply to the use of
per cent records for the convenience of teachers; yet it
must be remembered that nothing lies like figures when
used to indicate mental attainments. Especially so when
per cents are used as motives to study, and become an object
of attainment by the teacher. The work thus assumes a
formal character, and the higher the per cent the more
questionable the qualification. The more vigorous, original, and inquisitive the mind, the less capable and willing
is it to do routine, percentable work. A good class will
make a poor record when examined by a mechanical

routine teacher; while under the same conditions a poor class will make a good record. Class-honor men are not the men who take the honors in the real conflict of life. It is not the highest order of talent that consents to work for artificial ends by percentable products, nor such talent as most likely to succeed under such conditions. For this reason the comparative attainment of pupils, either in the same class or in different schools, cannot be ascertained by a study of per cent records. Before per cents can reveal the truth, it must be known how pupils have been taught, the kind of questions by which they have been tested, and the kind of teacher who makes the estimate. But let the teacher make the most of this unreliable arithmetic, so that it never be made the motive to study.

And in the same way examinations have their use and abuse. They may perhaps be properly used to ascertain the condition of a pupil's mind as a basis of instruction, but never as an impending danger to the careless and easy-going pupil. Yet the need of the examination as a test of knowledge is greatly overestimated. It is strange if the teacher who has taught the class does not, in so doing, learn their mental condition. Certainly the written recitation and the preparation of papers out of recitation time are an exact, searching, and sufficient test; all of which the natural course of instruction requires. If it be desirable to call this an examination, then let it be admitted that examinations are proper for purposes of instruction. After a class is well taught under normal conditions, it would be a serious confession on the part of the teacher to claim that an examination is needed to ascertain the condition of pupils' minds touching the subject taught.

It seems that college authorities have found no other solution of the distressing examination problem than that of surveillance or student-honor, as appears from an article by Professor Stevens in the February "Forum" of '95. It seems not to have occurred to them that the examination might formally disappear in the regular and matter-of-course daily work, and thus avoid its objectionable feature. When an examination has any other than an educative value, which reduces it to regular class work, it is the subtlest irony to speak of putting pupils on their honor; the fact of the examination is the challenge of honor, and is only a more refined surveillance, while purporting to be its opposite. The entrance examination might seem to be an exception to all this, since there has been no recitation to test qualification. But if the professor should state to the student what qualifications are necessary for successful work in the department, the rest may be left with the student; for he undertakes the work at his own peril, under the coming and all-sufficient test of ability to carry the class work. Students who would desire to deceive in this matter are too rare to justify imposing rules on the mass, and such are sure to be caught in due course of instruction.

But suppose examinations are needed: they cannot be relied on as anything more than a very inaccurate and partial test. This fact is well emphasized by Fitch. "Nevertheless we have to postulate here that there are certain very valuable qualities which are not revealed in a written examination, and which the habit of exclusively relying on such examination does not encourage. Except in so far as diligence and obedience are concerned, examinations do but little to test moral qualities, or active power. They do not tell you whether the action of the mind has been rapid or sluggish, nor how far the pupil has been influenced by a sense of duty or by strong interest in his work. Still less do they help to gauge those attributes on which success and honor in life so much depend, — sympathy with human beings, deference for superiors, the power of working with and influencing others, address, flexibility, manner. Let us once for all acknowledge that for either educational purposes, or for testing or selection, with a view to the requirements of a university or of the public service, the best examinations do not test the whole man, but leave some important element of character to be ascertained by other means; and we have still to ask, within what limits are examinations valuable, and how we can get the maximum of good out of them."

Be this as it may, there can be no question of the evil effects of the examination system as a means of enforcing industry and diligent perseverance in well-doing. The method of examination by which the student is induced to risk all on the last fearful moment, is vicious and demoralizing in the extreme; and for such a test there can be no apology, except that by a kind of military enforcement of work, study can be secured which clumsy teaching fails to realize. Some abnormal condition of things, such as

large, diverse membership of classes, may suggest the
need of testing by formal examinations; but certainly in
a well-ordered system no such necessity can arise. Then
shall we have examinations? Yes, continually. How?
As a regular organic part of the instruction, both oral and
written; and as a matter of course, pupils being unconscious that anything new or unusual is happening. Certainly never with the idea of external pressure to study,
entailing fear, dread, and nervous strain, — the very elements which have perpetuated the system. The matter
of breaking health through nervous strain is not an insig-
nificant part of the account; but still worse is the moral
strain, often too great to be borne. How frequently in
college work, where there is the most diligent detective
practice on the part of the professor, do we hear the
student chuckle at his exultant story of superior generalship in the war where cheating and lying are fair!

But all this is gradually passing, and the danger lies
in a more subtle form of evil. This is the same as that
pointed out in speaking of per cents, — namely, the disturbance of the natural and healthful tension of the mind
with the world of life and thought which it is to master.
It is the intrusion of foreign elements between the pupil's
present real self and his future ideal self, as found in the
world he is to study. If the elements of anxiety, fear,
the venturing of chances, and the temptation to deception
could be eliminated, and one still think of the examination
as a motive, it could not be used without turning the pupil
back upon himself; whereas the motive and the method

of the pupil's work must bring self-forgetful activity on the subject for consideration.   Self-realization is by the process of self-sacrifice.   Self-activity is the striving to be the other self, which is the thought and spirit of the world objective to the self.   This is the organic unity of consciousness which must be kept inviolate.   Self-activity must not be taught to practice deceit; the object acted on must be the motive in the action.   The teacher cannot use the examination as a motive to study without breaking faith with the mind's craving for unity with the world about it; nor without weakening the tension for that unity.   The hungering and thirsting of the soul for the righteous spirit of the world is the supreme ethical virtue; and it is this desire in some form to which every teaching act must appeal for its motive.   To make any other appeal is a perversion of the ethical relation of the pupil to the world in which he lives.

All other artificial stimulants are to be disposed of by the same argument as that used against per cents and examinations.   When a prize is offered the assumption is that the subject of study has not in itself sufficient inducement to its study; or that the teacher lacks skill in bringing the subject into stimulating touch with the mind of the learner.   Properly treated, the subject is its own prize; and to substitute any other is a subversion of the true method and motive in learning.   The prizes so generously offered to college students by well-meaning people, and distributed from the platform at commencements, are antagonistic to the spirit of true education.   It cultivates a longing and vain striving for ignoble things; and this in an institution pledged to liberal culture and the higher life of thought and sentiment. Emulation, a much-praised motive to study, is likewise prohibited both on ethical grounds and by the true method of learning. The pupil has only so much of total energy to expend on the subject; and why should some other fellow be thrust in the way to consume a part of that energy? The pupil has all he can do to rise above himself; and the standard of his achievement should not be located in another for the sake of excelling the other. He certainly should make a legitimate use of the other as a standard for himself; but rivalry, which has in it the desire to excel another for the sake of excelling him, needs to be refined out of the pupil rather than cultivated in him. Self-emulation is the only worthy emulation. Any other cultivates

> "The low desire, the base design,
> That makes another's virtues less;"

and also

> "The strife for triumph more than truth."

The use of such a motive may secure, through strife and contentions, a great display of animation and effort; but these are only feverish, fitful spasms from a disorder in the school organism, and not to be taken for genuine zeal and aspiration.

Thus always the ethical character of the organism is tested in the support given to the unity of the pupil with himself in the subject he studies. It must contain no element which stands counter to self-realization. Whatever be the pressure to make instruction effective, the organism must preserve its integrity, so as to secure wholesome living within it while the end of instruction is being sought. It permits no appeal to low desires and base motives; allows no insult to the pupil's rational desire for knowledge, nor to the world of life and reason which are sufficient to gratify that desire. In order to the growth and health of the body, the appropriate activities are prompted by the unerring desire for food, air, warmth, light, and action. Is it not fair to assume that the growth of the mind has been equally well insured by some impulse which prompts to acts appropriate to its growth? The abiding passion of the soul is for knowledge, and all the teacher can properly do is to take this fact fairly and at its worth. This passion he may stimulate, make definite, and attach to the proper objects; but he cannot introduce a substitute without weakening the life-giving connection between the pupil learning and the object being learned. This duty of appeal to proper motives is well enforced by Thomas Davidson in the "Forum," on "The Ideal Education of an American Boy."

"In all his teachings, moreover, he [the tutor] will take the utmost care never to let his pupils think that they are studying merely in order to pass an examination, but always to make them feel that the only end of study is complete autonomous manhood. He will do his best to show them how, and in what degree, each study contributes to this end, so that they may never feel, as so many boys do at present, that they are studying merely because some one else wishes them to do so, and consequently, that their work is a slavish, unprofitable task. A boy who does not feel that every hour he spends in study is spent for the sake of the highest end he knows and desires, is in an immoral frame of mind, and by no means on the way toward moral autonomy. The greatest triumph as a tutor is to make his pupils feel that what he requires of them is the very best thing they could be doing. If he fails in this, he has virtually failed altogther; for every hour that a self-conscious being spends without feeling that it is bringing him nearer to the goal of his aspirations is an hour slavishly and unrighteously wasted."

Influence of Social Combination. — Having guarded the purity and integrity of the organism by rejecting all harmful agencies, it is free to enter into positive ethical training. School life is the transition from the family to the larger complex social life of the world. In the pupil's little school world he is trained to the forms and habits of life which fit him for the larger social world of which he must soon be a member.

Society is infinitely complex, yet a closely integrated whole; and the fundamental law of social life requires that the individual conduct himself so as to preserve intact the social whole: not in a merely negative sense, but in that of active co-operation to worthy achievements of the race. The great obstacle to proper social conduct is the inability of the individual to grasp adequately the bewildering complexity of society into a closely integrated system of human effort for personal welfare. Concrete experience in family life, the most elementary social unit, develops in the child the germ of the organic conception, which is to be finally expanded, by the school and other agencies, into a comprehension of the complex life of the social whole. In school, which carries over into itself much of the family spirit, this germ of social conception becomes definite and complex through the more varied and exacting requirements of school life. The school, as the pupil meets it, is a concrete, comprehensible social world, — an object both to be observed by him and of which he is a living part; and, if properly managed, becomes a most potent influence in forming proper habits and sentiments of social life.

Whatever training the school gives preparatory to social life, is based on the fact that each pupil pursues his work in association with others. This fact is the basis for a criticism frequently made against public school education, — namely, that of evil associations and corrupting influences of vicious pupils. But this has the counter-balancing benefit of bringing the evil under the influence of the good; and from the standpoint of the whole the standard of virtue may not be lowered, leaving ground for complaint only with those parents whose children are, or are thought to be, above the average. However this may be, the school society, under proper regulations, is certainly better than what the child will probably be thrown into as he approaches maturity. With a well-regulated system, and proper vigilance on the part of the teacher, the social tone of the school may be made elevating even to the average pupil. Being alarmed at certain specific forms of contagious vice, we are too prone to leave out of the account contagious forms of virtue, as well as the general toning influences of a well-ordered school. At any rate the school is not at fault, for the life of the school as a whole is as good as the material sent to it, and out of which it is made. All that need be urged upon the school as an institution is that it be so thoroughly organized and managed to the end of higher life and conduct, as to be above the general standard of social life, in which the pupil, while out of school, would probably be moving.

People must come in touch; it is impossible to save by secluding and stowing away in pure corners of the earth. To hide from the world till evil disappears is a poor way to attain to the crowning glory of virtue, — the overcoming of evil. Holiness is not the absence of evil, but the victory over it. A school may be so managed as to corrupt morals and manners, and to foster a sense of disorder, injustice, and anarchy; but this only suggests a potency for good in the opposite direction, both of which facts make doubly strong the necessity for the teacher keeping clearly in mind the leading social virtues which a well-managed school cultivates.

The first of these virtues, which arises from the mere fact of school association, is that of : —

Politeness. — Society, in its popular sense, is only a general expression for the recognized kinship and community of life among individuals. In some degree the world as a whole is a sociable world; for man recognizes man in every form of human life, and expresses the recognition in customary social forms. In no situation in life is man relieved from acknowledging that every other "is a man for a' that." Thus society, in its most intangible unity, is bound together by the universal sentiment of community of life in the race.

This mere feeling of unity finds expression in the social amenities and courtesies of life. Such recognition, not the outer form but the inner spirit, is true politeness. This is a chief social trait, because it is that quality of one's actions which acknowledges the ideal, potential self in another; and from which arises the unity of the social whole. Impoliteness is the treating and greeting of another by reference to his shortcomings; and the true test of politeness is found in the adjustment of actions to the ideal and potential when these are obscured by vice and degradation. It is easy enough to be polite to kings and queens,—to real kings and queens in spiritual virtues; but true politeness discerns the king and queen in every one, — even in the loathsome leper begging before the castle gate of a knight-errant.

There is a vast difference between the true recognition of the ideal worth of another as man, and the mere formal and conventional use of politeness; yet the two are one in being based on the acceptance of the brotherhood of man. In any form, politeness is a means of maintaining social unity. Imagine each speaking and acting with reference to the real character of his associates, and at once society is dissolved into atoms — perhaps with bruises and bloodshed.

To test one's act as to politeness, it need only be asked whether it break the unity of good feeling binding together the social whole.

For instance, if one should meet an enemy in a social gathering, it would be impolite to treat him there as an enemy, because such conduct would break the unity and check the flow of social life. It is impolite to read a newspaper in church while the pastor is preaching, because he is thus treated as an unworthy pastor, and the congregational unity disturbed.

Politeness in school is only a phase of the law of organic unity in the school. Pupils must meet on a common plane, where each is forced to recognize the equal worth of others, in whatever uninviting guise it may appear. A dignified and well-toned system of management necessarily maintains strict practice of polite conduct as an indispensable means to the integrity of the organism. Thus the teacher does not need to turn aside to enforce polite conduct, but secures such conduct in due course of management itself. Whatever the teacher may do by way of instruction in the theory and practice of politeness should be done; but the practice of politeness is inherent in the organism itself. And whatever definite instruction may be desired on the subject, no better opportunity can be found than that furnished by the concrete situations of school life. As the pupil in all cases of discipline must reason out how certain acts destroy the school, so here he should see specifically how he disorganizes the school by impolite conduct. And then such conduct has still greater claims upon the individual on his own account; which should become so clear to him as to appeal to his sense of ideal worth, as well as to his respect for the ideal worth of another, and the desire for the welfare of the school as a whole.   The requirement of politeness put upon the teacher in maintaining unity in the class reciting has already been indicated.   This may now be taken as a general principle of securing unity in any form whatever. By the nature of the teacher's relation to his pupil, he must address himself to the ideal in the pupil.   When the teacher, in an angry moment, berates the pupil for his shortcomings, he subverts the very foundations of the school.   The weakness of a pupil can never be made the means of attack without risking disorganization.   At all times the teacher must see the lady or the gentleman in his pupil, even when brought to the necessity of dealing sternly with misdemeanors.   The school is still a phase of polite society, and the teacher must never violate social proprieties because occupying a position of authority. However wayward a pupil may be, he must receive the same social attention and courtesies as a perfect lady or gentleman.   Teachers, because they have not realized ideal politeness, may have to make a little effort to treat the uncouth and saucy boy with the same attention and courtesy as the well-bred and attractive one; but the law of unity permits nothing less; and in this the teacher finds, as does the pupil, rugged discipline in polite conduct.

On the general basis of sociable relations, the school

and society pass into more definite organic character by the parts assuming orderly arrangement with reference to work to be accomplished. This new fact requires of the social unit the ethical sense and habit of : —

Order. — The first condition to active co-operation of the parts of a mechanism or organism is that the parts be orderly disposed with reference to each other, — that each be in its proper place at the proper time. The essential element in order is that of punctuality, — the observance of time and place conditions of co-operation. The organ must be where it is needed when it is needed, or it is useless; therefore, disorder is disorganization.

The law of order involves the law of silence; for the individual must not simply be in body at the right time in the right place, but must be there in spirit also. His mind must be abstracted from everything but the work in hand; and this is the inward silence which produces the outward silence. Order requires attention to a given matter at the right time and place. A pupil is in order when his mind is at the point of doing the thing next to be done.

The school organism cannot move forward without placing the pupil under the strict requirement of order; hence, it again appears that the teacher need not turn aside to cultivate the ethical virtue in question, but must simply enforce as usual the law of unity inherent in the organism. Thus may be cultivated the habit of order and the feeling of obligation to the law, which are necessary to maintain unity in any phase of social organization. Social co-operation is impossible in any form without obedience to the law of order; and as civilization advances, and social phenomena become more complex, the more exacting is the requirement of the law. A railroad system would be instantly paralyzed by a failure of operatives to conform to the schedule; and the business of the whole country would be destroyed by absolute uncertainty as to the time and place of transactions. And such is the general necessity for order running through every phase of organic life; and also manifested with such mathematical precision in the world of physical law. The parts of the solar system are always in place and at their appointed task. And so should it be with every social organ; but such organs work by capricious will instead of by mathematical law, and must be trained to observe the first law of heaven. With such necessity of the moral virtue of order, and with such definite requirements made by the law of the school on that virtue, the school should be managed with the conscious purpose of forming habits of order, and of cultivating a quick sense of obligation to the requirements of the law.

The next social virtue arising after order, and which the school by its inherent structure cultivates, is that of : —

Truthfulness. — Truthfulness is essential not only to the integrity — the unbrokenness — of the individual, but to the integrity of an institution. The co-operative unity of the parts already orderly arranged is maintained through some form of communicating medium. Now truthfulness, including all forms of fair and honest dealing, is that quality in the communicating medium by which each knows the real intent of the other. Truthfulness is the transparency of the communicating medium. If this medium diffuses or refracts the real intention of the communicator, the recipient is thrown off the track, and his effort to join in the thought and work of the other defeated. Truthfulness in word or act brings two or more minds into unity; but lying and deceit sunder yet more widely, while pretending the opposite. Thus unity of thought and harmony of action rest, after order, on the transparency of the social medium of communication. Lying not only antagonizes truth, but cannot harmonize with itself; hence liars must have good memories. Any truth fits every other; while any lie fits no other, else it would be true to the lie it fits. Thus lying is the absolute destruction of organic unity.

Hence, truthfulness in school, especially between teacher and pupils, is an absolute requirement of the law of unity in school management. For instance, if the pupil in any way deceive the teacher as to what he knows about the subject of instruction, he so far dissolves organization with the teacher; and should the teacher cause the pupil to practice self-deception as to his real mental condition, the result is the same, with change of criminals. The true attitude of the pupil will reveal his whole mind to the teacher, especially his weakness, so that the teacher may render the needed assistance. But the teacher generally so puts the pressure on the student by threats, examinations, marks, prizes, and honors, that he is not only tempted to conceal his weakness, but to make a false show of knowledge. This is another root of the evil discussed under false incentives, which appears now as a thoroughly disorganizing element at the vital centre of the school, — unity of teacher and pupil. This suggests the care the teacher should exercise in keeping the mind of the pupil open as to its vital needs, both in order to secure the focal unity of the school and to avoid the cultivation of a most subtle form of deception, blighting to every phase of social life. But in every phase of school experience the teacher must bring the pupil to the practice of truthfulness; and he will not lack for opportunity to lead the pupil to discover the disorganizing character of deception and falsehood. The school is inherently true and honest; and the cultivation of these virtues requires only the rigid enforcement of its fundamental law.

The individuals of society, bound together by the mere feeling of community of life, and having assumed definite and orderly arrangement with reference to each other in the work to be done; and further, given to truthfulness in communication, the welfare of the school and of society requires yet another attribute, that of: —

Industry. — The individual, when organized into a system of work, must give steady attention to that work. The wheels of a machine cannot stop without stopping the machine; idleness is a social disorganizer, and not only because of the absence of labor, but because the dead, disjointed material becomes a burden to the social body. Whether viewed from the individual or social standpoint, idleness is immoral, — from the individual standpoint, because activity is the law of his being; from the social, because the whole is disintegrated when the activity of its members ceases. Industry, from the social point of view, is the tension of the activity of the individual with the movement of the whole. Industry is the very life and movement of any social organization; hence, idleness on the part of the teacher or pupils destroys the school to the extent of the idleness; and complete idleness is complete destruction. It is needless to urge that a school thoroughly organized and managed, with its regular, exact, and punctual requirement in performance of duty, is a most powerful means of bringing the pupil into the habit and spirit of industrial life. It is in the school that the pupil passes from capricious play to systematic and continuous effort to some end beyond that of mere activity itself. To make this transition from play to work effective, the work must carry with it the joy of play. In the highest art of labor, and in the most effective social industry, work has a reward in the activity itself. Work to the artist workman is as play to the child: in both there is the joy of free activity,— in the former the result, besides the activity, is a useful end; in the latter, there is no end beyond the activity itself. The philosophy of the kindergarten games and gifts is in the fact of transforming play into work, while still maintaining the reward of the activity in the activity itself. The public school, artfully managed, is the very institution to supply to society members who are not simply industrious by force of conviction and habit, but who have the joy of industry in the heart, — members who are free men in the love of wholesome labor, rather than slaves to the inexorable requirements of the hard industrial world.

> " Work thou for pleasure ; paint, or sing, or carve
> The thing thou lovest, though the body starve.
> Who works for glory misses oft the goal ;
> Who works for money carves his very soul.
> Work for the work's sake, then ; and it may be,
> That these things shall be added unto thee. "

In the pursuits of life under the law of industry, one individual will traverse the path of another, and come in conflict with him, unless restrained by a proper sense of the rights of others. Thus, the integrity and welfare of society further requires the cultivation of the restraining sense of : —

Justice. — As defined by Herbert Spencer, justice is the equal freedom of action; or, to put it in his own words, as found in his "Social Statics," in which, and also in his "Principles of Ethics," he has forcibly elaborated the doctrine: "Every man has freedom to do as he wills, provided he infringes not the equal freedom of any other man." In absence of the social relation of justice, neither the school nor any other institution, nor society as a whole, can maintain its organic life. Absolute injustice may readily be seen to be absolute disorganization. Pupils cannot invade the rights of each other, nor teacher and pupils make mutual invasions, without dissolution of the organism to the extent of the invasion. Hence, justice in the school is only another phase of the law of unity;

and to train pupils into the habit and sentiment of justice, the teacher need only to manage the school thoroughly with reference to its primary law.

How the pupil is thus required to practice justice is quite obvious. For instance, in order that class work may proceed, each pupil in the class must consider the rights of every other in the class, and subordinate his own caprices and desires to their good. In every case of self-regulation the welfare of the class is consulted, and the pupil must bring himself into line with that welfare. He puts the individual self down for the general good. And so it must be with reference to the school as a whole; the individual has many desires which are crossed by the requirements of the school as a whole. At every turn he must stop to consider what the good of the whole in the interests of its members requires of him. To that he must render obedience. This is a universal form of morality, — the putting down of an individual preference for a general good. Such is the requirement of virtuous citizenship. Patriotism — justice intensified — is the feeling which enables one to sacrifice self for the good of country and humanity. We have much to say about training for citizenship, and devise means through the study of civics and history to prepare for that duty. But no means ever devised is more potent than an efficient system of school management. Under this the pupil has the citizen's experience, — lives a real citizen's life. He is required to think his own conduct as a member of the little school-world, and is thus trained into citizenship habit. In the other way he merely theorizes about citizenship. It is not more or different studies needed in school in order to cultivate this virtue, but a more efficient system of school management. Civics in the blood is more vital than civics in the head. Especially unpromising is the newest method of teaching patriotism by the galvanic process of ritualism. Nothing but patriotic experience through the concrete situations of life can call forth the desired virtue. Pretence and formalism are death; while the altruistic demands made on the pupil in due course of a well-regulated school life are potent and healthful influences in the cultivation of a patriotic spirit.

And thus we have already passed from justice to the climax of school and social virtue, that of: —

Altruism. — Under this sentiment the individual does more than simply avoid interference with the rights of others, and now positively seeks their good. This, therefore, is the completely unifying social virtue. If all were dominated by an altruistic spirit, society would move forward as one harmonious whole. Hence, this is the virtue which in common thought and literature is exalted above every other; it is the chief glory of Him who went about doing good.

At the outset we found this to be the necessary attitude of the teacher towards his pupils; and without the same feeling of mutual helpfulness among pupils, school life would be dreary and incomplete. The kindergarten properly makes much of this spirit, and it is claimed that such is the fundamental basis of all school work. This

14

may well be accepted if we expand the idea of altruism to include all forms of self-forgetfulness in the spirit of the world lying objective to the pupil. In this larger sense altruism is the last word either in method of thought or of action. The highest principle of instruction already advocated in "The Philosophy of Teaching," and now presented in conclusion as the truest principle of management, is that of immediate self-forgetfulness in the environment of truth and life in which the pupil lives and moves and has his being.

The highest outcome of such an appeal to altruistic consciousness in both instruction and management is a realizing sense of the rational order of the universe; that there is reason and law above the individual to which he must bow assent, if he would realize his destiny. The school, beginning with the little concrete world immediately about the pupil, including the school itself, gradually opens his eyes to the fact that his own highest good is to be at one with the divine order of things. Gradually, and by long experience, it dawns upon him that the reason in the larger world about him is his reason, and that he must conform to this reason if he would achieve the highest good. He comes finally by habit and insight to seek the divine order of the world to make it his order.

And thus we are reminded that altruism is not an end, but only a method of thought and action; that while it is more blessed to give than to receive, one always receives more than he gives. We speak of cultivating the social virtues for the good of society; but society is an empty

abstraction apart from the concrete lives of the individuals. A social virtue is, after all, a personal and
private virtue. Kindness, gentleness, mercy, and lo
have more worth to the subject than to the object of th
But these have no meaning except in attachment to ot
and the only method of cultivating them is through
immediate consciousness of their object and not their subject. The practice of altruism returns as personal worth
in some form, else why be altruistic, if human worth is
the goal of education? The proximate end is certainly
another person or another truth; but the teacher, in training to practical knowledge and social virtues, should no
forget Kant's maxim: "So act as to consider every ma
as an end in himself, and never as a means only." Th
pupil must lose his life, but always in order to find it
Through efficient school management the pupil is required
to deny himself, to sacrifice himself, for the good of others
and the institution as a whole; but this is only his proper
subjective discipline, and the school as a whole is only
his own rational nature, at first unrecognized. So while
he, out of respect to others and devotion to the school,
practises politeness, order, truthfulness, industry, justice,
and love, his own life is being disciplined and enriched
by these virtues. All high achievement for self, as well
as for humanity, comes through a self-forgetful devotion
to a universal objective good; yet the ultimate test of
ethical training is its personal, private, and subjective
value. The ultimate test for management is the same as
that already set up for instruction in the "Philosophy of

Teaching," — namely, the self-realization of the individual, which is best explained by the words, rational ~edom, or the power to choose and live in the highest ~l. Hence, the ultimate ethical question for school ~gement is, how does the securing of unity to the end ~nstruction discipline to: —

Rational Freedom. — The law of the school requires ~ach pupil to bring himself into unity with the organization, and thus he must limit his customary, free, irresponsible conduct; must harmonize his actions with others, and direct his effort to serious worthy attainment.

When the child enters school, his actions are chiefly ~ntrolled by caprice. He has not been trained to sub~dinate his likes and his dislikes to the attainment of a ~tional object. In school for the first time, perhaps, he ~s held to systematic effort to attain some good beyond his immediate desires. By the nature of the school organization he is compelled to limit himself to a given task, at a ~iven time and place. No phase of school work is more beautiful, or more suggestive of educative power, than a school-room of children brought into the unity of an industrious effort to attain some worthy object. The very nature of the school requires self-limitation on the part of each pupil, and no form of training could be more directly in the line of moral habit and moral power. All forms of combination in school work help to enthrone reason and will above desire and caprice, — help to exalt the spiritual man above the natural man. The exact combination of a gymnastic exercise requires a high tension of will to control the body; and this strengthens the power of the soul to rule its naturalness. The ethical culture of gymnastic drill is of more value than its physical training.

Thus the nature of the school organization forces the pupil to self-limitation. But the pupil is not morally free until he needs no such specific external means to self-control. The school controls conduct in specific and minute ways; but through this control the pupil is gradually to grow stronger, so that he will, by and by, need less direct and immediate help from the organization, until at last he becomes wise enough to set up his own law of conduct, and strong enough to render obedience without the help of master and machinery. As a result of school discipline, the pupil should be enabled, in the light of reason, to set up his own standard of action, and by habit and strength of will to bring himself under the law thus set up. It will be here recalled by the reader that the plan of management discussed in the preceding pages, with the view of securing the unity essential to instruction, is exactly in line with that of securing the ethical freedom of conduct here noted. At all stages of his course the student is to explain the reason for a given course of action, and then to make his decision in favor of the line indicated. The pupil must thus be released gradually from obedience to mere authority. The teacher must take pains to put the pupil under his own guidance. The teacher controls too much, leaving too little for the pupil. For the child sitting by the stove to move, without permis-

sion, because too warm, is better than to move with permission. Under such circumstances pupils are sometimes
ordered back to remain until they get permission from
headquarters. The pupil then raises the hand; the teacher
nods consent; then matters are in good condition because
the pupil has rendered obedience to authority. But such
obedience confers no power of self-direction; whereas
such power would be cultivated if the pupil debate the
question and decide for himself. This idea of obedience
to a teacher is full of mischief. The pupil should obey
the law inherent in the case, which he himself is able to
expound and set up as his only master. In an important
sense, the pupil should do as he pleases. The teacher
must let him alone, and watch his actions and tendencies.
Suppose a pupil in the primary room should go to the
water-pail three times during a recitation, would it not be
well to let him go without interruption; and then during
the day, at some convenient time, — unless too much going,
make an immediate demand, — to have a general discussion as to how long a pupil can do without water before
suffering; and whether, if a pupil's wants have all been
supplied before the beginning of a recitation, he could
suffer before the close? And then permit pupils to point
out the interruption occasioned if all should thus frequently visit the water-pail. Personal mention of the
offender need not be made, but he should be drawn into
the discussion. Or, if thought best, he alone might
discuss the matter with the teacher. No matter about
details; I mean only to insist that the student be led to

set up his own standard of action and make his own decision in regard to it, so far as possible, without any regard for the mere authority of the teacher.

This reminds one that there are two kinds of disciplinarians, — one who, by the force of authority, maintains the appearance of good order; the other causes good order to arise within the pupil. What often passes for good order is quite the opposite; and the so-called good disciplinarian secures only the temporary form of discipline. This is the heavy-handed drill master who, by force, may quell a mob, but who can never prevent the occurrence of one. And, too, the appearance of order is good only while pupils are in the immediate presence of the master. No teacher is worthy the name of disciplinarian who does not strengthen the pupil to govern himself after he turns the corner of the school-house. An able-bodied man may crush a school into fearful silence, which is the worst of disorder; but the teacher — and such may be a timid lady — who can cause order to originate in the understanding and consent of the pupil, whether securing the same beautiful and formal external appearance or not, is the true disciplinarian. A majority of teachers, from the common school to the college president, who have been noted for disciplinary power, have gained their notoriety on the score of external crushing power over the student. And by this I do not mean the application of physical force; there are a thousand and one ways of intimidating and bribing a student into the semblance of good conduct. The pupil may be enticed with rewards, roll of honor, good will of teacher, and divers kinds of favors; or threatened with loss of privileges, with demerits, with lowering of grades; with whatever rack and torture desperate ingenuity can devise. I know what proud success teachers report to have achieved by this, that, and the other disciplinary device of fear or favor; but, beneath the surface, it surely can be but a questionable success. It may be that a teacher must hold the fort temporarily by such external forces; but he should be ashamed to report success till the pupils see the reason of proper conduct as grounded in the school itself, and voluntarily make the law of the school the law of their behavior.

The true disciplinary power of school management is well illustrated in the method of punishment, already discussed. Suppose the young lady who communicates in school be kept in to make up lost time; or that the time be doubled, and still multiplied until it becomes so unpleasant that she finally desists. It has been shown that unity in such a case is not secured; for the unity desired is in the will of the student. While apparently at one with the school, she is not really so; for to be so she must purpose with the school. But more important still, such a method of procedure fails to cultivate the power of rational self-control. If she had been required, as insisted on in preceding pages, to explain the law inherent in the school against such conduct, and then to take charge of herself in the light of the law, the temporary end of management would not only have been more effectively secured, but there would have been a gain in general power to rule the spirit in the light of reason. Every time the pupil is led to resolve that he will take charge of himself, the teacher has accomplished a victory for righteousness. This is a daily and almost hourly opportunity. The whole spirit of management, and prominently that of punishment, requires constantly just such a resolution. Thus the true means of securing unity as a condition to instruction is the true means of ethical discipline.

And thus in every phase of school management, the pupil is led to adopt reason and law as the guide to conduct; and through this is disciplined to the power of choosing the highest good, the true self, as against the claims of the lower nature. Such supremacy of the higher over the lower self comes from the intelligent and free adoption by the pupil of the school as his own rational nature objectified. The school's inherent laws of politeness, order, truthfulness, industry, justice, and love, are his own requirements of the school; and these return into his own life through his obedience to them in a form which he himself, without at first discerning it, projects. In the development of the fundamental law of management it was argued that the school is well managed and firmly grounded only through the pupil's conscious adoption of it as his school, — as the projection of his own rational needs. This fact now appears as the fundamental harmony of the whole process, in that the same adoption is the essential feature in the process of ethical training. As at the outset, we saw the school evolving out of the requirements of the pupil's own nature, so now we see it dissolving as ethical elements into the life whence it came. Hence, school management secures, aside from instruction, the self-realization of the pupil through his unity with the rational nature of the school; and from this, through unity with the law and reason of the world into which the school leads; which reason, law, and order will, too, gradually appear as his true other self; so that he can but know that to realize his destiny he must conform to the divine spirit and order of the world, as manifested in nature and life everywhere about him.

Thus every institution becomes a constant appeal to his true nature; the kingdom of heaven is seen to be the realization of the divine life of the individual. And thus, too, by extension, the world becomes a reflection of the individual; the heavens which declare the glory of God, declare also his glory; everything becomes a pillar of cloud by day, and a pillar of fire by night to lead the individual out of the Egyptian bondage of his lower nature into the realm of spiritual life and freedom.

> "Over our manhood bend the skies;
>   Against our fallen and traitor lives
> The great winds utter prophecies;
>   With our faint heart the mountain strives;
> Its arms outstretched, the druid wood
>   Waits with its benedicite;
> And to our age's drowsy blood
>   Still shouts the inspiring sea."

INDEX.

ANNOUNCEMENTS

SOCIAL EDUCATION

By COLIN ALEXANDER SCOTT

Head of the Department of Psychology, Boston Normal School

12mo.   xi + 300 pages.   List price, $1.25 ; mailing price, $1.35

SOCIAL EDUCATION is a handbook for teachers who think. It is a plain and practical account of the life of the school from the standpoint of the social forces which are ever at work among pupils of all ages. It is not based upon mere ideals or philosophical abstractions but upon countless observations of schools of various kinds from the kindergarten up to the college grades. It is not the child as a separate individual, but children as they are actually found in classes and groups in and out of the school, which form the principal subject of discussion. The book is full of the actual activities of living children, and its aim is to show how these can be made more productive, more ethical, and more happy and spontaneous, — not sacrificing, but promoting and intensifying thereby, the scholarship and the truest discipline of the school.

> Mr. Colin A. Scott's careful study of Social Education leaves its readers duly impressed with the supreme and overwhelming importance of understanding the child at every step of his career, of making his citizenship date from his school days, of molding him, through the principle of organization, into an active and intelligent member of the state. The book is sincere, earnest, ardent. There is no flaw to be found in its reasoning. We wish Dr. Keate could have had the advantage of reading it before he became head master of the Eaton School. — *Life*.

GINN AND COMPANY PUBLISHERS

AMONG COUNTRY SCHOOLS

By O. J. KERN
Superintendent of Schools, Winnebago County, Illinois

12mo. Cloth. 366 pages. Illustrated. List price, $1.25; mailing price, $1.35

THE author's endeavor in preparing this work has been to create a new ideal in the training of the country child.

The book is the result of seven years of very earnest thought and hard work in an endeavor to secure for the country child his rights so far as an educational opportunity is concerned. The country school should have that freedom which country life affords. This book has but little to say about the mechanics of school management.

In the training of children and the development of character no greater opportunity can be offered than that now presented to the teacher in the country school. The author hopes that this book will prove suggestive to the teacher and school officer who are striving for the spiritualization of country life through the medium of the school. He believes that a careful reading of its pages will show a practical way of interesting the "farm child through farm topics."

Some of the chapter titles, indicating the suggestions given in this distinctly novel treatise, are :

THE RIGHTS OF THE COUNTRY CHILD
OUTDOOR ART — BEAUTIFYING SCHOOL GROUNDS
INDOOR ART AND DECORATION
A FARMER BOY'S EXPERIMENT CLUB
THE COUNTRY SCHOOL AND THE FARMERS' INSTITUTE

GINN & COMPANY Publishers